THE

ORIGIN AND PROGRESS

OF THE

AMERICAN PARTY
IN POLITICS:

EMBRACING A COMPLETE

HISTORY OF THE PHILADELPHIA RIOTS

IN MAY AND JULY, 1844,

WITH A FULL DESCRIPTION OF THE

GREAT AMERICAN PROCESSION

OF JULY FOURTH,

AND A REFUTATION OF THE ARGUMENTS FOUNDED ON THE CHARGES OF

𝔑𝔢𝔩𝔦𝔤𝔦𝔬𝔲𝔰 𝔓𝔯𝔬𝔰𝔠𝔯𝔦𝔭𝔱𝔦𝔬𝔫 𝔞𝔫𝔡 𝔖𝔢𝔠𝔯𝔢𝔱 𝔆𝔬𝔪𝔟𝔦𝔫𝔞𝔱𝔦𝔬𝔫𝔰.

BY JOHN HANCOCK LEE.

BOOKS FOR LIBRARIES PRESS
FREEPORT, NEW YORK

First Published 1855
Reprinted 1970

STANDARD BOOK NUMBER:
8369-5334-7

LIBRARY OF CONGRESS CATALOG CARD NUMBER:
79-117881

PRINTED IN THE UNITED STATES OF AMERICA

TO

ALL AMERICANS,

THIS WORK

IS RESPECTFULLY DEDICATED

BY

THE AUTHOR.

(3)

PREFACE.

No apology is needed for the publication of this volume. The history it purports to give embraces an account of some of the most important events that have ever transpired in Philadelphia. These are but imperfectly understood by many of our immediate citizens; much less by those living at a distance. The rise and progress, principles and intentions, past doings and present condition of the American political party, have been most grossly misrepresented by opposing partisan presses. Great care has been taken not only to suppress the truth, but to convey false impressions to the minds of those who have had no other means of information. It seems proper that these errors should be corrected, and the facts, as they really occurred and now exist, given as wide a circulation as possible. Thousands of good people in all parts of the American Union, have even yet to learn that the original members of American associations were neither rioters, murderers, nor church-burners; but orderly and peace-

1 *   (5)

loving citizens; associated for laudable purposes,
actuated by pure motives, and labouring for the promotion of the true and best interests of their country.
They have simply aimed to arrest, by laudable and
lawful means, the growing evils that were too palpably
manifest through the influence of combinations of
naturalized citizens, in our political institutions. To
this end alone the American associations were formed,
and are now maintained.

In describing the terrible disturbances in Kensington and Southwark, as mild language has been employed as the circumstances require, and truth and
honesty will permit. It would be neither profitable
nor expedient, at this late day, to speak as plainly concerning certain prominent actors in those scenes as
their injudicious and even reprehensible conduct would
have justified. Enough is said to place that portion
of our subject in a proper light.

Let nothing that is herein written be construed into
an attack upon the religious tenets of the Catholic
church. This is no place for such a discussion. Our
history demanded a statement of the indisputable facts,
that the political conduct of certain portions of the
Catholic community provoked the American opposition, and that riotous members of that church were
the originators and reckless prosecutors of the Ken-

sington and Southwark disturbances. With the doctrines of the church we have nothing to do; nor would
we utter a harsh sentence against the peaceable and
respectable portion of its communicants. Among these
are some of the writer's nearest and best friends, and
better citizens or purer-minded Christians are not to
be found. The improper counsels of certain clergymen are condemned; and had they been of any other
sect, and acted in the same manner, they would have
been as severely censured.

The interference of naturalized citizens, especially
the Irish, with our elections, and their elevation to
offices of trust and profit, which should be filled by
Americans only, are treated with as much tenderness
as such subjects deserve; nor has the foolish encouragement that the American people have given to foreign
arts and artists, manufactures and manufacturers, been
too roughly handled. The writer is so far an American in feeling, as to imagine his own country prefer-
able to any other in the world; and rejoices to observe
a growing disposition on the part of Americans to give
that patronage and encouragement to valuable American productions, which they have been wont to lavish
so freely upon worthless importations.

CONTENTS.

(9)

HISTORY

OF

THE AMERICAN PARTY.

CHAPTER I.

Necessity for the establishment of American Associations—Outrages of
Foreigners at the Elections—Aspirations for office of Naturalized Citizens—Meeting of native Americans at Germantown in 1837—Their
Constitution—Organization of the First American Republican Association in Spring Garden—Similar associations formed in various wards
of the City and County.

THE necessity for establishing American political
associations in the large cities of the United States
had been seriously felt many years before any active
or efficient measures were adopted to that effect. The
rapid influx of foreigners into the country, and the
facility with which their votes could be secured by
political wire-pullers, had become the subject of most
serious consideration, and of no little alarm. It was
well known that the Naturalization Laws, even as they
then existed, were a mere dead letter, and that men
were yearly brought to the polls, and their votes
received, who had not been sufficiently long in the
country to have lost the odour of the steerage of the

2   (13)

ships that brought them across the Atlantic. This was not all. Such men were exceedingly active at the elections—were noisy and riotous—and actually drove away in disgust many native citizens. Outrages of this kind were frequent, and encouraged and applauded by party leaders and aspiring demagogues. These latter cared not by what means they obtained office and power, and none were more available or cheap than these newly-arrived immigrants, especially the Irish. The hooks with which these were caught were baited with promises of the minor offices, all of which they were rapidly beginning to fill. It so happened, however, that they were not altogether satisfied with petty positions; they began to feel their importance, and to make demands of those who had used them for tools, that excited some little alarm. The babe, that had lain quiet in its cradle, had grown up to manhood, and its gigantic body was no longer to be easily managed. The servant aspired to be the master. A large number of honest citizens looked on aghast. They saw approaching dangers, and determined, if possible, to avert the threatening evils. The party leaders were helpless, and, like wretched gamesters, were daily increasing their stakes, with a desperate hope of getting "even in the end." They were playing a losing game.

Such was the condition of things, when, in the year 1837, a large meeting of native Americans was held in Germantown, Philadelphia County, for the purpose of discussing the subject of the rapidly increasing evils, and the means best calculated for their remedy. At this meeting the following Preamble and Constitution were adopted with great unanimity, and ordered to be published. Similar meetings were held, and similar declarations made about the same time in New York City, where the foreign influence had assumed even a more threatening aspect than in Philadelphia.

PREAMBLE AND CONSTITUTION.

On the 4th of July, 1776, our forefathers proclaimed to the world the independence of these United States, and the equal right of all its citizens to the free and fair pursuit of happiness: on that day they affixed their names to that document, the most illustrious ever penned by the hand of man, and pledged 'their lives, their fortunes, and their sacred honour,' to the support of the same.

In 1790, a law for the encouragement of emigration was enacted, holding out certain inducements to the foreigner to come and make his abode amongst us ; among others, he is entitled, after five years' residence, to the right of suffrage, and thereby a representation in our councils. Of this we are now convened to complain., While, at the same time, we invite the stranger, worn down by oppression at home, to come and share with us the blessings of our native land—here find an asylum for his distress, and partake of the plenty a kind Providence has so bountifully given us, we deny his right (hereby meaning as foreigner any emigrant who may hereafter arrive in our country) to have a voice in our legislative halls, his eligibility to office under any circumstances, and we ask a repeal of that Naturalization Law, which, it must be apparent to every reflecting mind, to every true son of America, has now become an evil. This we ask not so much for ourselves, as for our children. It needs no logic to prove how rapidly increasing is the foreign influence, even now by far too powerful in our country; and the day must come, and, we fear, is not far distant, when most of our offices will be held by foreigners—men who have no sympathy with the spirit of our institutions, who have never sacrificed aught to procure the blessings they enjoy, and instead of governing ourselves, as is our native-born right, we shall be governed by men, many of whom, but a few short years previously, scarcely knew of our existence. Is this the way to secure and perpetuate the freedom for which our ancestors bled and died? No, Americans, no! Let us come forward then, and prove that the spirit of '76 is not yet extinct, and that we are not degenerate sons of worthy sires. Let us crush this rising power: it has already blossomed, let us destroy it in the bud, ere the fruit reach maturity.

We have said that this law was an evil. At the present moment it is particularly so; for Europe is industriously ridding herself of an excess of population now become burdensome to her. And whom does she send? Her paupers, her convicts, the outpourings of her almshouses and jails. Even lately has a would-be-regicide been landed on your shores by a national vessel. We beseech you, by the shades of the heroes of the Revolution, to blot out this foul stain from our 'scutcheon, and leave the field as pure and bright as ever. The emigrants from Europe are principally of that class who, discontented and oppressed at home, leave there, filled with all the requisite materials to spread among our citizens anarchy, radicalism, and rebellion. Greedy of power, and regardless of civil restraint, they come to the land consecrated by the blood of our ancestors, ignorant of our customs, caring nothing for our laws, and strangers to all those essential qualities so necessary in self-government, and so indispensable to our existence as a free and happy people.

Now, honestly and seriously entertaining the opinion that, by a repeal of the Naturalization Law, all the foregoing evils, with many others, would be removed, and believing that this object can never be effected by either of the great political parties of the day, singly, we, the American-born citizens of Germantown township, and its vicinity, without any distinction as to political creed or religious faith, do unite together in an association to co-operate with all other similar institutions of native Americans, in order to obtain a repeal of the Naturalization Law, by all honourable means in our power."

This laudable movement at Germantown was not followed up with sufficient vigour, and the American cause was temporarily abandoned. Its honest projectors were incapable of coping with the political chicanery of the experienced wire-pullers, log-rollers, and pipe-layers of the old parties, and these were again left to fight their own battles, undisturbed by any outside interference. With them the strife was simply for the spoils of office, and the results of the election depended upon which were willing to pay the highest price for the still increasing foreign vote. It was felt on all sides that the balance of power was now held in that vote, and it was by no means so easily procured as in former years; hence it was not only a bone of contention, but a formidable shilalah that gave many sound raps upon the heads that snarled and fought around it.

In the mean time, very many of the native Americans, who were free from party trammels, had taken the alarm and determined to arrest the progress of the growing evil. Hence, in the early part of December, 1843, a respectable meeting was convened at a hall on the Ridge Road, in the district of Spring Garden, in the present city of Philadelphia. At this meeting the subject of the undue influence and misused privileges of the foreign population was discussed at considerable length, and with great ability. After gravely and maturely deliberating upon the matter,

2 *

the convention resolved that the speedy adoption of
efficient measures to counteract the influence of the
evils considered was necessary to secure and perpetuate
the dearest rights of American citizenship. This, it
was maintained, could only be accomplished by the
organization of a new political party. Hence a society
was at once formed, and designated " *The American
Republican Association of Second Ward, Spring
Garden.*" The subject was about the same time
agitated by a number of the citizens of Locust Ward,
in the city ; and a similar association was organized
in that ward in the month of January ensuing. In
North Mulberry and Cedar Wards, associations of
the same character, and aiming at the same objects,
were soon after established. These organizations were
followed in rapid succession by others, until in a very
few months an American Republican Association, embracing many of the most intelligent and respectable
citizens, sprang into existence in almost every ward
throughout the city and county. Never did a movement, commenced with so little noise, parade and
show, commend itself so forcibly to the understandings
and better feelings of the people. As though the
hand of Providence were in the work, directing and
controlling it, the measures of the new party met with
the general approbation of all who were not governed
by opposing political party principles, or blinded by
the misrepresentations of those whose interests depended upon arresting the progress of the principles
of the new associations. As the friends of the new
measures, day after day, continued rapidly to increase,

their enemies, becoming alarmed, grew louder and more violent in their opposition, and more perverse in their misrepresentations. The contemptuous sneers with which the assumed futility of such an undertaking was at first treated, soon gave place to harsh and ungenerous denunciations, and even threats of violence and destruction. But in despite of all opposition, the cause continued to move steadily and successfully onward, and from present indications is destined to prosper still, until it shall swallow up all other principles of civil government in our country, and the objects at which it aims be most perfectly accomplished.

CHAPTER II.

Declaration of Principles—Unanimity with which they were adopted—
Existing evils demanding a Remedy—Alteration of the Naturalization
Laws—The Bible in the Public Schools—Union of Church and State.
—Americans only should execute the Laws.

THE general rising up of the people at that period
to organize a new political party, and form associations for the prosecution of its measures, is a matter
no less remarkable than the unanimity with which they
agreed upon the adoption of a declaration of principles.
On this point, there appears to have been but little,
if any, difference of opinion. This singular concurrence of sentiment, however, not only established the
fact that certain grievances did really exist, but it
pointed directly to the nature of those grievances, and
exhibited the only evident means through which an
efficient remedy could be applied. A few dissatisfied
individuals might arise in the community, and cry out
loudly and complainingly against seeming evils or imagined wrongs; but such a body of men, of different
occupations, opposing political sentiments, conflicting
religious opinions, jarring interests, and even with personal animosities, as that which composed the American party, never united together to contend against
imaginary evils or remove grievances which had not
become too palpable to be doubted, and too oppressive
to be longer tolerated or endured. And when these men,
scattered all over our city and county, were seen lay-

(20)

ing aside every other consideration—their political and religious prejudices and personal enmities—and uniting together in a common cause, they gave the clearest and most positive evidence that there existed a powerful and irresistible necessity for their united movement. Let this marvellous union continue to subsist, (and it is now hourly increasing in strength and numbers), this people must succeed in all their efforts, and accomplish all for which they contend. With perhaps several exceptions, in which trifling unimportant alterations have been made, the following is the Declaration of Principles approved and adopted by all the early American Republican Associations:

1st. We maintain that the naturalization laws should be so altered as to require of all foreigners, who may hereafter arrive in this country, a residence of twenty-one years, before granting them the privilege of the elective franchise; but at the same time, we distinctly declare that it is not our intention to interfere with the vested rights of any citizen, or lay any obstruction in the way of foreigners obtaining a livelihood or acquiring property in this country; but, on the contrary, we would grant them the right to purchase, hold, and transfer property, and to enjoy and participate in all the benefits of our country (except that of voting and holding office), as soon as they declare their intentions to become citizens.

2d. We maintain that the Bible, without note or comment, is not sectarian—that it is the fountain-head of morality and all good government, and should be used in our public schools as a reading book.

3d. We are opposed to a union of church and state in any and every form.

4th. We hold that native Americans, only, should be appointed to office, to legislate, administer, or execute the laws of their own country.

It is no part of our object to enter into a lengthy
defence of the principles here set forth. They speak
for themselves. They are true, just, and such as
American citizens have an unquestionable right to support. They infringe upon the rights of none. They
deprive no man of privileges which are his due. And
they are, in all respects, such as we should suppose
every citizen who loves his country, and desires its
welfare more than his own personal exaltation, would
cordially embrace and manfully maintain. While they
grant to all foreigners the rights and privileges
guarantied to them by our constitution and laws,—
while they disclaim any intention to interfere with
their opportunities to acquire property and enjoy the
blessings of our country—they declare a self-evident
truth, one, which, if no other argument could be offered
for its maintenance, has been demonstrated by the
disregard of all law exhibited by the Irish in Kensington, in their repeated savage attacks upon American
meetings, that our elective franchise has been held too
cheap—that our naturalization laws are faulty—that
foreigners are not prepared to perform all the offices
of citizenship as soon as they land upon our shores—
that five years are not sufficient thus to qualify them
—and that a longer residence in our country should
be demanded, before they are permitted to occupy
stations and exercise powers which they are not qualified
to fulfil or properly direct. In maintaining this position, it will be seen that its advocates wished not to
interfere in any way with foreigners who were already
residing in our country. Many of these had become

naturalized citizens, and all the privileges and rights of American freemen had been granted them. With these the principles of the new party had nothing to do. No desire had ever been expressed to take from them, or in any way to lessen, these privileges and rights. So far as the elective franchise is concerned, it was only upon foreigners who may hereafter visit our shores, and settle on our land, that the principles of the American party were intended and are calculated to bear. And that party was organized because it was important and necessary that such should not obtain so cheaply and so readily the benefits of American citizenship, as did those who had previously settled in our midst.

This explanation, though not necessarily connected with our narrative, seemed required to correct the false impression which had industriously been circulated, that the new party aimed to deprive foreigners of rights which had been guarantied to them by our constitution and laws. So long as the constitution and laws remain unaltered, foreigners will continue to experience all the benefits which they now enjoy. But should the new party succeed in effecting one great object of its organization, viz. : the alteration of the naturalization laws, so as to require a residence of twenty-one years in our country to entitle a man to the privilege of the elective franchise, or the entire repeal of those laws, then foreigners who have not yet settled here will have no more claim to that privilege in less time than twenty-one years, than they now have in less time than five years. So that the principles

which the new party advocates, no more interfere
with the rights of foreigners, than do the present
existing laws of the nation.

In regard to the declaration "that native Americans
only, should be appointed to office, to legislate, administer, or execute the laws of their own country,"
we have heard no plausible reason assigned why it
should be denounced as either unreasonable or unjust.
But if it were a mere unsupported matter of opinion,
surely every American citizen has a perfect right, not
only to the enjoyment but the open expression of that
opinion. And if he chooses to give his influence
and vote in favour of Americans, in preference to all
others, to fill the offices of government, he cannot
truly be accused of arrogating to himself any unjust
prerogative, or of interfering with other men's privileges. It is a privilege we enjoy to bestow our favours
upon those who in our own judgment are most worthy
to receive them ; and we pray that the time may never
come when we shall be deprived of this privilege
and be made the subjects of rulers not of our own
choice ! And while we feel at liberty to demand this
for ourselves, we have no desire to exclude any others
from its enjoyment. We freely admit that naturalized
foreigners enjoy it to the same extent that we do
ourselves. They have a right,—an unquestionable
right,—to select their own rulers. We have no wish
to deprive them of that right. Let them enjoy and
exercise it. Let them maintain it upon the housetops,
if they please, and at all the corners of the streets.
Let them determine to vote for no man to fill an office

in our country who is not a naturalized citizen. Let
them advocate this principle in our public prints, and
hold town meetings for its dissemination and support.
We shall not interfere. We shall not even complain.

3

CHAPTER III.

As the American party continued to increase in numbers, the leaders of the old political associations grew more and more concerned about their prospects of success at the coming elections. Both whigs and democrats had been confident of electing their own candidates; and in the height of their pleasing anticipations and exultings, it was not a matter of surprise that they should become alarmed at the rapidly increasing strength of a new organization which had almost spontaneously sprung up, and suddenly and unexpectedly threatened to supplant them both, and thus blast all their cheering hopes. A new enemy had crossed their paths, and was about to frustrate all their long-cherished and well-contrived plans for office-seeking, which had already obtained an importance no less unaccountable than mortifying. They had been too much engaged in the warfare with each other, to give very close attention to the new party or the objects of its organization. They had all along regarded the matter as ephemeral and insignificant, and went on as usual, wheedling and coaxing the naturalized citizens, and sycophantically bargaining for their

suffrage.   Suddenly, however, they awakened from
their dream of safety, and opened their eyes to the
danger that threatened from the quarter they had
despised.   The little speck in the political firmament
had swelled into an immense cloud, and portended a
storm of no trifling moment.   Their ships were evidently in danger, and they commenced in earnest to
cast loose their sheets and halyards, and furl and reef
and trim their sails.   They were bad sailors, and suffered
material damage from their ignorance and awkward-
ness.   Each party at first supposed the new movement
to be a mere trick of the opposition to carry the elections, by deceiving with a few plausible pretences some
of their unwary friends into the enemy's ranks.   Hence,
at the same time, both whig and democratic papers
commenced a violent outcry against the American
party.   Whig editors cautioned whigs to beware not
to lend it their influence, nor be cajoled into its measures, for it was a democratic contrivance to weaken
their strength; while democratic publishers were no
less positive in denouncing it as a wily scheme of the
whigs to destroy the power of democracy.

The one was as correct in its opinions as was the
other.   Both were alike mistaken.   Neither could
conceive it possible for the new party to be governed
by *pure motives*.   This, with them, seemed to be a
matter entirely beyond the reach of possibility.
Honesty or purity in politics was a thing of which they
were incapable of forming any conception.   It was
utterly at variance with all their notions of party tactics.   And hence it was some time before they could

be made to feel that the adoption of the new principles was neither a *whig* nor a *democratic* TRICK, but the prosecution of an honest determination of American citizens, uncontaminated by the chicanery of aspiring politicians, and superior to the debasing influence of purely party feeling, to correct the evils and destroy the corruptions which had crept in among both of the great parties and was threatening the destruction of the civil liberties of the people, and the hallowed institutions of our government.   But this fact could not be concealed from the great mass of the native citizens ; and the disinterested, the untrammelled, the purest and the best of both democrats and whigs, continued to throw aside their party feelings and prejudices, and gather around the standard erected by the American Republican Associations.

The first attempt to defeat the cause of the new party having failed, another effort was made, which for a time promised better success.   It was well understood with what tenacity men cling to their religious opinions, and that to interfere with their rights of conscience in regard to their religious faith and practice, is emphatically to " touch the apple of their eye." This feeling, so prevalent among all Christian denominations, was greedily seized upon by the enemies of the new party, as affording a fair opportunity of arresting its wide-spreading influence, by fastening upon it the charge of *religious proscription, intolerance, and persecution!* a charge which, as will eventually appear, has been the cause of much dreadful mischief. This charge, so false and unfounded, was attempted

to be established by the second and third articles of
the declaration of principles, published in the preceding
chapter. The declaration that " we are opposed to a
union of church and state," was said to be an assault
upon the Catholic church, and an evident attempt to
deprive Catholics of the liberty of conscience. But how,
or why, has not yet been made to appear. Do the oppo-
sers of the American associations wish it to be understood that Catholics are *not* opposed to a union of
church and state—that they are really aiming at such a
union—and that by contending against it, an attempt
is made to deprive them of the liberty of conscience
in matters of religion? What other inference can be
drawn from the premise here assumed? If it be so,
that this *is* an object of the Catholic denomination,
and of none other, then the declaration in question
pinches hard upon Catholicism; but if Catholics have
never entertained such an opinion, the declaration certainly has no more to do with them than with any
sect of Protestants. Though the extreme sensitive-
ness of Catholics upon this subject is well calculated
to excite suspicions unfavourable to them, we freely
acknowledge that it is not sufficiently conclusive to
warrant a direct charge of evil intentions.

But it was furthermore maintained that in affirming
the Bible to be a proper book to be read in our public
schools, and in persisting in the reading of it there,
the new party are justly chargeable with religious proscription and intolerance towards the Catholic portion
of the community. Indeed! Has it really come to

3 *

that? Is the Protestant version of the scriptures so exceedingly offensive to the Catholics? What are the obnoxious sentiments it contains, which being read in the hearing of Catholic children, subjects them to danger, and the reader to the charge of intolerance and persecution? We have never discovered anything in that book, the reading of which we could suppose would injure the morals of either Catholic children or their parents! And the probability is, that had they been carefully instructed in its readings, we should not have had to lament the death of our citizens who were so ferociously murdered in our streets by Catholic bigots. But even did the book contain sentiments objectionable in their character, we cannot perceive that even Catholics would be proscribed or persecuted by its being read in our public schools. Their children are not compelled to listen to its instructions; and even if they were, they have only to be assured that the book is Protestant, to be guarded effectually against any influence it may have upon their minds. Besides, our citizens have a perfect right to order what books they please to be read in the public schools: and he who would deny that right is unworthy the name of a republican. And so far as the Catholics are concerned, no one can doubt what course they would pursue had they the predominance in our country. Not only the Protestant Bible, but every other Protestant book would be rejected from our schools, and none but Catholic publications would find a place within their walls. And should the time ever come when they do obtain that predomi-

nance, and pursue that course, we shall never raise
the hue and cry of persecution; for it would be just
what we would expect, and what we have every
reason to believe they will leave no means untried to
accomplish.

The charge, therefore, of religious intolerance and
proscription, not being supported by the Declaration
of Principles of the American party, that charge
cannot in truth be urged. It originated with wily
politicians, whose opportunities for political advancement were being endangered, and was, doubtless, first
put forth, for the only purpose of bringing into dis-
repute the new party, and of thus destroying its
increasing influence. And well would it have been for
the deluded Catholics, had they more clearly understood the motives which originated this charge, and
the objects for which it was advanced. They would
not, perhaps, have become the willing dupes of the
designing, or the suffering victims of their own folly
and unbridled passions. Urged on, however, by those
who either knew not, or cared not into what dreadful
excesses they were capable of plunging, they have
turned public sympathy, which they hoped to obtain
in their favour, the opposite way, and rendered themselves unworthy of the confidence they have received,
and the subjects of the most bitter prejudices and
injurious suspicions. And far off must be that day
when they shall regain that high position which they
have heretofore occupied among American freemen.

There is another fact which properly comes in here,
connected with this portion of our subject, well

worthy the consideration of the public. It is not only true that there is nothing in the Declaration of Principles of the American party, to justify the charge against them of religious proscription; but it is also true that the advocates of those principles who were connected with the organized associations, almost uniformly protested, in their speeches and through the press, against any disposition to interfere in any way with the religious rights or opinions of others. That disposition was again and again disclaimed by the American speakers, in a series of debates which were held in the lecture room of the Philadelphia Museum. It was frequently condemned in the ward and mass and other meetings of the new organization. And it was from its very commencement disavowed in the columns of the "Native American" newspaper, by its editor and contributors.

But even had the case been otherwise, and the new party organized expressly to circumvent and oppose the Catholic influence that was too palpably being exercised over our elections, they would not only have been engaged in a justifiable but a laudable work, and the Irish Catholics, and their leaders, tutors and deceivers, were the last that should have raised the cry of religious proscription or persecution. They had for years been provoking just such an opposition. They were not satisfied to see their magnificent temples of worship springing up like magic in every part of the land, and crowded with devotees of their religious creed; they must needs employ those very temples and those very crowds to obtain political and temporal power. And by these means, and these alone, they not unfrequently succeeded in elevating to high municipal and government positions, men who had been but a short time in the country, who had nothing to commend them but their religious faith, and who were utterly incompetent to fulfil the duties of the responsible stations they had reached. Such was emphatically the case before, and it would be audacity on the part of any one to deny that it has been the case since the establishment of the American party.

The New York Herald, of May 10th, 1844, in speaking of the disturbances in Kensington, made the following remarks applicable to this portion of our subject. They are strictly true, directly to the purpose, and worthy of preservation. It is scarcely necessary to say that Archbishop John Hughes, of the Catholic church, is the reverend gentleman to whom allusion is made:

"The first thing which strikes us in examining these events, is the introduction of religious elements into what seem to have preceded the whole of the outrages. It was not a mere quarrel between opposing political factions. In the conflicts of party in this country, there has often been great excitement, and very violent war of opinion, but we have never, on any former occasion, witnessed the infusion of such a degree of bitterness as led to the perpetration of wholesale murder, or wide-spread destruction of property, as we have seen in this terrible outbreak in Philadelphia. Political contests have presented a more dignified character, and confined themselves to the more reputable weapons of reason, discussion, argument, and common sense. It is the infusion of religious prejudices into political contests that prepares the way for outrage, disorder, blood, tumult, and conflagrations. Of this we have now witnessed the melancholy evidences in Philadelphia. And of the existence of the same elements of danger we have also had evidence in the course of the last election in the city of Brooklyn.

" Who then first introduced this desolating element of religious prejudice and religious feeling into political contests ? On whom rests this fearful responsibility ? Who first raked together the embers of religious animosity, and opened the way for the perpetration of those bloody and devastating outrages ? Let us come to the root of the evil. Let us trace it to its origin; let us discover who have been the authors of this deplorable state of things, that they may receive the odium which they deserve.

"Well, in looking back upon the history of the last few years, we find that there was a certain assemblage of politicians, of a particular class, in what is called ' Carroll Hall,' and that a Rt. Rev. Bishop of this city, abandoning his holy calling, went down into that arena and harangued the assembled multitude in relation to their political duties at the election of 1841. This holy man, had he been left to follow the impulses of his own heart and the precepts of his Divine Master, would never have thought of wandering into that arena, or of exhibiting himself in that character. But we have every reason to believe that he was misled, and betrayed, and duped into that conduct by some paltry politicians, for the mere political purposes of the election of the day.   Here, then, was the first introduction of the religious element into political contests."

CHAPTER IV.

Hostile spirit manifested toward the American Party—The Sign of the
Ball in Second Ward, Spring Garden—Meeting at the Commissioners'
Hall, Moyamensing—Interference of an Irish Commissioner—
Weavers' Riots—Disturbance at the Polls in Spring Garden—Threats
of violence at the Chinese Museum.

IN this chapter we shall simply present the reader
with a few specimens of the hostile spirit exhibited
toward the Americans previous to the more violent
manifestations which resulted in so great a sacrifice of
life and property in Kensington. The public, or a
great part of it, have laboured under the impression
that prior to the Kensington riots the party had been
entirely unmolested; but the truth is, it had been
abused on a number of former occasions, and had submitted with a degree of patience and forbearance
rarely shown under similar circumstances.

It has already been remarked, that the first association was organized in the Second Ward, Spring
Garden. This association held its regular meetings
in a hall on the Ridge Road, known as the "Sign of
the Ball." This name was derived from the fact of a
large ball being hung in front of the building, which
being transparent, was illuminated on the evenings of
the association meetings. This ball, though perfectly
harmless in itself, did not fail to excite the indignation
of the enemies of the American cause. They indeed

(36)

did not need much to excite that indignation, and
hence, for want of something better at which to fire it
off, it was let loose in the discharge of musket shot
through the unoffending ball.   This outrage, though it
did no material damage, afforded some little evidence
of the belligerent disposition of the opposition, and
was a sort of forerunner of greater violence to come.
Well would it have been had they satisfied themselves
with firing at the ball, instead of making marks of
human bodies upon which to try their skill at shooting.

But their restless spirits were not to be so easily
quieted, nor their determined hostility so soon to be
satisfied.   There appeared to be an eager looking
after opportunities for wreaking an unprovoked vengeance upon the advocates of the new principles.
Hence, when in February, notice was given that a
meeting was about to be held in the Second Ward,
Moyamensing, for the purpose of organizing an American Association in that district, declarations were
boldly and liberally made that no meeting of the kind
should there be held.   It is needless to say that these
threats came from that portion of the inhabitants who
held the dominancy there, who had for some time con-
trolled the elections, and who in their own country,
across the great waters, never aspired to govern themselves, much less the freemen of America.   Yet, notwithstanding these indications, the meeting was held in
the Commissioners' Hall, and was permitted to pass
off far more quietly under the circumstances than
there was reason to expect.   An attempt was made to
interfere with the proceedings by a noisy Irishman,

4

who was well known, but the disturbance amounted to nothing of a serious character, from the fact that others whose assistance he probably anticipated, concluded that it was better to keep the peace, in consequence of the unexpectedly large number of persons who had assembled.

This fact, which was highly gratifying to every lover of peace and order, was not so pleasing to other portions of the community. And *one of the Commissioners* of Moyamensing, by birth a foreigner, demanded to know *"who had the audacity"* to give up the Hall for the use of *Native Americans!!* Who will pretend to say, in view of such facts, that there was not cause for the organization of the American party, and a determined and persevering maintenance of its principles? Who, fifty years ago, would have supposed, that a newly imported foreigner would dare to question the right of American freemen to occupy their own public halls for the purposes for which they were erected? And who can doubt that the spirit which so authoritatively demanded an answer to this arrogant question, in that early stage of the American cause, was the same which, at a still later period, denied with stones and rifle balls the right of peaceable citizens to assemble for the expression of their political opinions, even in an open and unoccupied portion of our soil, in one of our most populous towns? When such men rule our country, we must submit to be more degraded than were they before they left their native shores to seek refuge and freedom on ours.

This, however, was not the most violent demonstration against the American Republicans, by their foreign opponents. Shortly after the above narrated events occurred, another district became the scene of an outrage, similar, though not to the same extent, as that which happened in 1834, in the northern part of the town, when on an election day, the Irish weavers of Kensington and Spring Garden, with their blue sticks, drove American citizens from the polls.

On the 15th of March, at an election in Spring Garden, the Americans were assaulted at the polls, and the common method of the lower classes of Irishmen—a resort to brute force—was employed to drive them off, and thus deprive them of one of the privileges of citizenship. In this disturbance, which at one time threatened to be alarming, one man was severely injured. Thus, it will be perceived that the destructive disposition of the Kensington rioters was no new thing. It did not spring up suddenly in that district, as some of the venal presses would have made it appear, in consequence of the inflammatory speeches of American speakers; but it had been imbibed and was tenderly nursed, long before the progress of the new party had reached that neighbourhood. Nay, it was born with its possessors in the Emerald Isle, and has been again and again exhibited *there*, in the ferocious and savage feuds with which the history of that country abounds, and its people have so frequently been disgraced.

This ferocious disposition was manifested in a striking manner on another occasion, to which reference may here profitably be made. Mention was made in another place of debates in the Philadelphia Museum. These debates were commenced in the month of February, and continued from night to night for some considerable time. They originated with certain political gentlemen opposed to the principles of the American party; and the question discussed, inquired whether foreigners were entitled to equal rights with American-born citizens? This question was controverted by a number of persons, of every political complexion, and with considerable ability upon both sides. But during its progress several blustering and exceedingly noisy Irishmen were permitted to take the stand and address the assembly, a great proportion of which was composed of their own countrymen. The violence of these speakers was a subject for regret and censure by the more reflecting and sober-minded of all parties. One of these men, who had been but a short time in our country, in the midst of the most inflammatory speech to which 'we ever listened, loudly and ferociously declared, that if the native Americans persisted in their determination to deprive foreigners of any rights which they claimed for themselves, they (the Irishmen) *would with the bowie knife and rifle demand and maintain those rights!!* And the thundering applause with which this declaration was received, told too plainly the approbation it met from his no less ferocious and lawless countrymen! We listened in amazement! We believed not that a man would have dared in such a place, to utter such a sentiment. Little did we suppose that hundreds could be found to applaud it so loudly! Much less did we

imagine the speaker to be in earnest, and his threat so
soon to be fulfilled!—that in so short a time the hostile knife would indeed glisten in the sunbeams—the
sharp crack of the rifle be heard in our streets, and
the swift and destructive bullet pierce the very hearts
of our countrymen!

CHAPTER V.

ASSOCIATIONS of American Republicans having been duly formed in almost all the other wards in the city and county, the American citizens of Third Ward, Kensington, resolved to organize an association in that ward also, and accordingly gave the usual notice for a meeting to be held for the purpose, on an evening in the latter part of April, 1844, at the house of Mr. John Gee, in Second Street, above Phœnix. On assembling at the place and time appointed, the citizens were informed that the intended meeting could not be held in that house, in consequence of certain violent threats which had been made and widely circulated, that any house in the ward which should be used for the purpose of holding an American meeting, would be burned to the ground. The proprietor of the establishment was satisfied that these threats were not idly made, but that a settled determination pervaded the riotous inhabitants of the district, to execute them to the very letter. He remembered full well the weavers' riots, the negro riots, the railroad riots, resulting in

(42)

the burning of the railroad depot in Front street, and was fully qualified to judge correctly the lawless character of the men who threatened the destruction of his own property. It was hence determined by the persons assembled to adjourn to another ward, and they accordingly repaired to a house in the Second Ward, where their meeting was held in peace. Here we have an instance of atrocity without a parallel in the history of our country. Never before were the citizens of any ward compelled to hold their political meetings in a ward adjoining, to escape the fury of a foreign rabble, who, although they had sworn allegiance to our laws, were the most daring, insolent, and reckless violaters of those laws of any who had ever received their protection and enjoyed their privileges. And the very oaths of allegiance which they had taken, and which they have insolently boasted make them better citizens than the natives of the land, being thus utterly disregarded, hold them forth to the world as perjured traitors to the country whose protection they had sought, and whose privileges they so basely abused. The truckling presses which looked to Irish influence to sustain their miserably sickly and dying existence, and sought every opportunity and occasion to cast reproach upon the Americans for the abominations which had been perpetrated in Kensington, never dared to publish the circumstances attending this first gross and unprovoked outrage upon the rights of citizenship, much less attempt to furnish an apology for the recreants by whom it was perpetrated! This language may have the appearance of severity; but it is not more severe than the nature of the case demands. Look at all the circumstances, and the admission must be made, that the unblushing effrontery and lawless determination of their Irish opponents are as highly censurable, as was the unparalleled forbearance of the injured American citizens deserving of the commendation and applause of every friend of peace and good order! And yet there were those from whom better things might have been expected, vile enough to approve the former, and condemn the proceedings of the latter of these two parties!

Other meetings of the Third Ward were afterwards held within the limits of the Second Ward. Invitations were extended to gentlemen in the city to address these meetings, who refused to comply, on the ground of their not being held in their proper place. This induced the members of the Third Ward Association to make another effort to hold a meeting in their own ward, and accordingly they published the following notice in the "Native American" of the 2d and 3d of May:

" A Meeting of the Native Born Citizens of the Third Ward, Kensington, was held on Monday evening, the 29th ult. After electing officers, they adjourned to meet in mass meeting on Friday afternoon, May 3, at 6 o'clock, at the corner of Second and Master streets. All friendly to the cause are invited to attend. WM. CRAIG, Prest.
JOHN McMANUS, Sec'y."

Agreeably to the above notice, a number of native

Americans assembled on the open lot adjoining the public school house at the corner of Master and Second streets. Their meeting was organized, and they proceeded to transact their business in a peaceable and quiet manner. Mr. S. R. Kramer, publisher of the "Native American," was called upon to address the assembly, which was small, and had taken the stand in answer to that call, and commenced an explanation of the principles of the new party, when suddenly a number of foreigners rushed forward, assailed the meeting with shouts, hootings, and clubs, and drove away its members in confusion, without the slightest attempt at forcible resistance. The stand of the speaker was torn from under his feet, and the staging demolished. The assailants, on this occasion, were Irish Catholics, and a priest of the Catholic church had left the vicinity within an hour previous to the attack. We make no comment upon this fact. The reader is left to decide whether his influence, if exerted, might not have prevented this shameful breach of peace and daring violation of the law.

Having been thus forcibly driven from the place of meeting, the Americans repaired to the George Fox Temperance Hall, where they again organized by appointing Mr. William Craig, Chairman, and Mr. John McManus, Secretary. The meeting was addressed in an able and spirited manner, by Mr. Longacre of Spring Garden, to the evident satisfaction of the citizens present. After which the following preamble and resolutions were unanimously adopted:

" WHEREAS, The citizens of Kensington have been violently assailed and maltreated at a meeting called for the expression of their opinions on public policy, and for the declaration of their feelings, and have, in pursuance of this same violent spirit, been driven by outcry and clubs from the place designated for their meeting—therefore

" *Resolved*, That we, the citizens of Kensington, in mass meeting assembled, do solemnly protest against this flagrant violation of the rights of American citizens, and call upon our fellow citizens at large, to visit with their indignation and reproach the outbreak of a vindictive, anti-republican spirit manifested by a portion of the alien population of Third Ward, Kensington.

" *Resolved*, That in view of the above transaction, we invite our fellow citizens at large to attend the next meeting, to sustain us in the expression of our opinions.

" *Resolved*, That when we adjourn we adjourn to meet in mass meeting on Monday afternoon, at 4 o'clock, at the corner of Second and Master streets."

The following extract from the "Public Ledger," of May 7th, in reference to the disturbances above related, as well as the more serious ones to be described in the next chapter, contain remarks of sufficient value to merit a place in these pages. Every rational and honest man will agree with the editor in the opinion he expresses. There were other public journalists of that day less disposed to speak the truth.

" No one will hesitate to say that the native American party having called a public meeting, had a perfect right to carry on their proceedings in peace, undisturbed by any persons, and that the disturbance they met with from persons opposed to the objects of the meeting, was as gross an outrage as was ever perpetrated upon the rights of any body of free citizens. The citizens who composed the meeting were assembled in the exercise of a right which is guarantied to them by the constitution, and it has come to a pretty pass if, availing themselves of their constitutional rights, they are to be assailed by others, and their lives sacrificed in the streets.

" They were assembled by public call, their object being a perfectly legal one, and the presumption is that those who were opposed to the meeting were attracted there from some mischievous motive. They were not embraced in the call; they could have had no proper object in being present at or in the neighbourhood of the meeting; and the consequences which resulted, indicate very plainly the folly, if not to say the wickedness of their designs, in going in numbers to the place. The presumption that mischief was intended is confirmed by the conduct of a reckless set of ruffians, who, a few evenings before, broke up a meeting assembled for a similar purpose. Such conduct as this is not to be tolerated with impunity in any country, much less in ours, where the hand of fellowship and good feeling has always been extended to the emigrant from other shores, and political equality so liberally offered them.

" It is a poor return for these favours if they are to turn round and strike at the liberty and rights of those who have so generously given them the power to do so. The circumstances which occurred yesterday are to be deeply deplored, both on account of the bold attempt to interfere with and abridge the rights of American citizens, and on account of the persons themselves who are charged with the act, against whom, judging from the nature of men, a determined hostility will be waged, and upon whom the effects of their own folly will be made terribly to recoil."

CHAPTER VI.

Mass Meeting at the corner of Second and Master streets—The speakers
—Provoking conduct of Irish carters—A storm—Adjournment to the
market-house—Murderous assault—Death of George Shiffler—A fight
—Names of the wounded—Conduct of Irish women.

In conformity to the resolution adopted at the
meeting of the preceding Friday evening, about four
thousand citizens assembled in mass meeting, on
Monday afternoon, May 6th, at 4 o'clock, on an
unoccupied lot, at the corner of Second and Master
streets. This lot was about one hundred feet wide and
one hundred and fifty feet in length, and was bounded
on the west side by the public school-house, which
fronted on Master street. The staging for the officers
and speakers was erected about the centre of the
west side of the lot, against the school-house fence.
The whole extent of the lot was covered with persons
who had assembled to participate in the proceedings.
The meeting was organized in the usual way, and
several gentlemen were called upon to address the
assembled multitude. Mr. S. R. Kramer, General
Peter Sken Smith, and Dr. John H. Gihon successively took the stand; neither of them, however,
occupying over ten minutes' time. Their addresses
were mild in character, and contained nothing against
which the most scrupulous could have reasonably
objected. While these gentlemen were speaking,

several Irish carters came driving their carts into the lot, and forced their way through the crowd, nearly up to the speakers' stand, greatly annoying the people, and even exposing them to danger. Each of these carts contained something more than an ordinary wheelbarrow load of yellow dirt which was brought there at that particular time, in that singular manner, and in such small quantities, for no good reason which has yet been assigned. Five or six of these diminutive loads were successively brought in, and emptied in the midst of the crowd, as near to the staging as the drivers could conveniently force their carts. These loads of dirt laid some months afterwards upon the spot where they were then thrown. They were not needed there at that particular time ; neither was any use subsequently made of them. *Neither of them was brought in until the meeting had assembled, nor was one sent there after the assembly had dismissed!* And when it is understood, that at the very time when these carters were committing this inexcusable outrage upon the meeting, there were assembled in the market-house, running parallel with Second street, on the north side of Master street, and a few yards west of the schoolhouse, a number of Irishmen opposed to the meeting, armed with fire-arms and other offensive weapons, none can for an instant doubt, that these carters were sent there for the purpose of provoking an attack upon themselves, and of thus furnishing a plausible pretext for an assault in return upon the meeting, on the part of their friends in the market-house, and the surrounding buildings. There was evidently in all

this a cunningly devised plan for the perpetration of a
premeditated outrage, for the consummation of which
the most careful preparation had been made.

But that Divine Providence which often takes the
wicked in his own craftiness, and guards the innocent
from harm, interposed to avert the calamity which
then pended over the American cause. Had the
carters to whom allusion has been made, been assailed
with violence by the assembled people, a fearful and
dreadful slaughter, far more extensive than that which
really occurred, would have ensued. For in this spot
the citizens were entirely unprotected. They were
surrounded by the residences of their enemies, from
whose windows a murderous fire could have been discharged upon them; and as they fled in the only
direction which could have promised security, toward
the market-house, they would have been met by the
assassins who there remained concealed, awaiting a
signal for the commencement of their work of death.
Then, too, it would have been exceedingly difficult to
have made it appear, that the Americans were not the
aggressors, and that their assailants were not only
acting upon the defensive, but for the protection of
their worthy friends, the carters. Had this scheme succeeded, the cause of Americanism would have received
a blow from which it could not have recovered; and
anarchy, and misrule, and brutal violence, would have
triumphed over order, law, justice, and right. But,
we repeat, the hand of Providence was here interposed
to prevent the evil threatened. For, at the moment
when the conduct of the carters was growing insuffer-

able, and a slight demonstration of a disposition at interference was being manifested, Mr. Lewis C. Levin was called to the stand. This circumstance restored tranquillity for the space of a minute. But the moment that gentleman commenced his remarks, before a solitary sentiment had been concluded by him, and before the subject of the carts had again drawn off the people's attention, the clouds which had been gathering for some time in the heavens, seemed suddenly to concentrate immediately over head, and discharged their overburthened contents in a torrent of rain upon the assembled multitude. For a second there was a pause, which was followed by a simultaneous rush for shelter in the market-house. This sudden and heavy fall of rain frustrated the wily designs of the enemies of the American party, and brought about a series of events which have turned the tide of popular feeling in their favour, and convinced the honest, the disinterested, and the reflecting of the community, of the correctness of their cause, the purity of their motives, the peacefulness of their intentions, and the growing necessity for the maintenance of their principles !

So sudden and unexpected was this movement, that those of the Irish who were waiting some provocation for an attack upon the meeting, were confused and undetermined in regard to their further proceedings. The most of them, as the crowd rushed into the market, retreated to a row of buildings, consisting of a hose-house and the dwellings of themselves and friends, situated in Cadwalader street, and facing the market-house, at the distance, perhaps, of some two

hundred feet.   Others, but their number was few, remained to contest the right of the citizens to the use
of the market.   This market-house had previously
been employed as a sort of rendezvous for the mobs
during the railroad and weavers' riots, which had previously disgraced that neighbourhood, and they seemed
to consider themselves solely entitled to its use.   An
attempt was here made to re-organize the meeting, but
the few Irishmen who had now mingled with the multitude of citizens, were determined that the organization should not take place.   They produced the utmost
noise and confusion, whenever any effort was made to
speak on the part of Mr. Levin, who had again arisen
to continue his address, and so constant and violent
was the uproar that it was impossible for that gentleman to be heard even by those who occupied places
nearest to him.

Among the most noisy of those who were now in-
terrupting the proceedings of the meeting, was an ath-
letic Irishman near the speaker, who brandished his
naked arms above the heads of those around him, and
swore terrible vengeance upon every one who should
dare to come into contact with his clenched fists.   So
exceedingly violent was this man's conduct, that some
person at length attempted to eject him from the
market-house.   A scuffle ensued between the two.
The Irish rioter drew his antagonist to the outer side
of the market, which fronted the dwellings and the
hose-house of which mention has been made, when a
stone was thrown from a party in the vicinity of the
hose-house, with tremendous violence, toward the

5 *

market, which struck with great force against one of the stalls. This was instantly followed by the discharge of a musket from the same direction. A pistol was then fired in the midst of those who had by this time taken sides with the men who had commenced the fight in the market, which seriously wounded in the face one Patrick Fisher, an Irishman, though favourable to the American cause, and who had previously been a constable in that district. A scene of confusion and strife now took place which beggars all description. The first impulse of those in the market was to rush upon the party near the hose-house who first assailed them, which they did, driving them off in every direction. But no sooner were they thus drawn out from the shelter of the market, upon the open space in front, and their open assailants dispersed, than a destructive fire was opened upon them with fowling-pieces, rifles and muskets, from the roofs, windows, loopholes, yards and alleys of the houses in front, which was kept up without intermission, until the ground was vacated by the American party. During this firing the utmost consternation prevailed, and men were shot down while endeavouring to escape from the scene of danger, without knowing from whence their injuries were received, so cautiously were their enemies concealed.

One young man, about nineteen years of age, was engaged throughout the afternoon, in supporting the American flag, which hung over the speakers' stand. This rendered him an especial mark for the aim of the enemies of the cause he was maintaining. Two or three times had the flag fallen to the ground, and as often did George Shiffler, with the assistance of several others, again raise it, and cause its stripes and stars to float above their heads. But his efforts were unavailing; for a bullet at length pierced his heart, and he fell as senseless as the flag he supported, to the ground. He was carried to the store of an apothecary near by, where in a few minutes he ceased to exist, and before the sun had gone down the lifeless body of the boy was laid at the feet of a widowed and distracted mother, who had centred her hopes of comfort in old age upon him, and who had left her but a few hours before, in the buoyancy and strength of healthful youth and happy expectancy. The flag which he had supported was torn and levelled with the dust, by those who had sworn to protect our country and her laws. And he and others were murdered by men who were pretending to love and revere and contend for the religion of Him, all whose teachings aim for the promotion of peace and good will toward man.

While the greater portion of the assailed party precipitately fled for protection, others remained to contest the ground with the ruffians who had so ruthlessly attacked them. Unarmed as they were, they gave battle, with brickbats and stones, to the miserable beings who were still firing upon them from the windows, alleys, and even house-tops, in the neighbourhood. This unequal warfare continued more than an hour, during which time, besides Shiffler having been killed, eleven persons of the American party were severely wounded. These wounds were inflicted mostly

with shot, bullets, and principally slugs, discharged from
the guns of the assailants. About a half dozen slugs,
together with a large quantity of shot, entered the
breast of Shiffler. The names of the wounded, so far
as was ascertained, were Patrick Fisher, Edward Spain,
Samuel Beatty, Charles Vanstavoren, Lawrence Cox,
Henry Temper, Thomas Ford, William Springer, John
Deal, George McAllister, and David Ford. None of
these wounds proved mortal. Others were severely
injured from the throwing of stones, brickbats, and
other missiles. It is not certain whether any very
serious wounds were inflicted upon the Irish Catholics,
who were the attacking party. After the first outbreak, they rushed into their houses, where they were
comparatively secure from danger. Several of them,
before they escaped, were somewhat injured. One
large man was observed to throw in rapid succession
several brickbats, with tremendous force, at a young
man who stood against the side of the market, who
suddenly stooped, and picking one up which fell directly at his feet, returned it with great violence : it
struck the Irishman on the forehead, and he fell senseless to the earth. He was afterwards carried away by
his friends. After the Irish sought refuge in their
houses, they could have suffered very little damage
other than that which was done to the property they
occupied. The Hibernia Hose-House, from the rear
of which the firing commenced, and nearly every
house from which shots were fired, was attacked, and
the windows and doors broken and destroyed, with
stones that were thrown from the excited and enraged

crowd. But stones and brickbats were comparatively harmless weapons with which to contend against the constant discharge of fire-arms, in the hands of concealed, well fortified, and desperate foes ; and hence, even the assaults made upon the buildings of the Irish were soon ended. The conduct of the Irish women in the early part of this battle, was no less fierce than was that of the men; for they were seen urging the men on to deeds of violence, and running in all directions, with their aprons filled with stones, rendering all the assistance in their power. One woman was knocked down with a brickbat, but she instantly regained her feet, and shouted at the top of her voice for the men to maintain their ground and give it to the natives. Thus commenced and thus ended the first battle between the Americans and the Irish Catholics of Kensington; well would it have been, perhaps, had it been the last.

CHAPTER VII.

THERE was one remarkable circumstance connected
with the lamentable occurrences just related, that
deserves something more than a passing notice, as it
illustrates in a most forcible manner the absolute necessity for the movement of the American party at that
day, as well as the continued maintenance of its principles in the present. At the period of which we write,
the aspirants for county offices looked to and depended
upon the Irish Catholic vote. Without it they knew
all hopes of an election were vain and fruitless. And
hence political demagogues were exceedingly tender
in their regard to the Irish master spirits who could
control that vote. These men had great political
influence in the county—could bargain and sell—and
even dictate terms to the leading politicians. It is
one of the evil and disastrous effects of this condition
of things to which we are about to refer. In the very
commencement of the outrages recorded, several citizens hastened with all possible despatch to inform the
sheriff of the county of what was transpiring, and to

obtain his official aid to quell the disturbance. They found him dining at the residence of a friend, and not over-much pleased with being disturbed in so agreeable an occupation. After much persuasion, however, he quietly took a seat in a cab and rode to the residence of the police magistrate of Kensington, an Irishman, who possessed as much influence almost over the Irish Catholics as did the priest, and decidedly more than the sheriff. After a brief consultation the sheriff returned to his cab and was driven back to the city, leaving the belligerents at full liberty to continue their work of destruction. But, although very many people were disposed to censure the sheriff with much severity, neither of the contending parties had cause to complain of his not giving them abundant opportunity to act out their pleasure. Had a limited civil force appeared upon the ground of the riot at the time when application was first made to the sheriff, the disturbance could readily have been ended, the *real aggressors* arrested, the peace of the neighbourhood restored, and the lamentable occurrences yet to record, prevented. But such a force was not employed. It was evidently believed that the Irish party had the strong cards in their hands, and it was determined that they should win the game if they could. The destruction of Americanism was the stake for which they played: and what was the value of a few lives compared with the accomplishment of this grand object? This was most essential to the preservation of a power most important to political demagogues, and one which must not be lost without more than an ordinary struggle. To this end deep plans had been laid, and, at whatever sacrifice, those plans were to be carried out. It would have been a desperate and dangerous matter for certain parties just then to have arrested the original rioters and the foreign murderers of native citizens. Those men possessed secrets worth knowing, and which it would have been exceeding bad policy to have exposed. Some of them were mere *paupers, beggars, half-naked starvelings.* Yet they held in their hands *costly guns and rifles,*—new from the manufacturers' shops,—and were provided with ammunition which money had been expended to purchase! Who bought those guns? Who furnished those rifles? Who provided that ammunition? Not the poor wretches who used them! These had scarcely bread to eat! They were without sufficient clothing to cover their nakedness! They had no money to buy arms, powder, and shot. They were the mere *tools*, the working machines, of other and more responsible parties. Why, then, should they have been arrested? Why place them in a position where they would have been compelled to disclose some most unpleasant truths? The sword of justice that would have fallen on their necks, would have severed from their shoulders wiser and more precious heads! And then the hated and despised American party would have triumphed!

After the frightful scenes of Monday afternoon, the Americans gathered together early in the evening in mass meeting, at the Assembly Buildings, corner of Tenth and Chestnut Streets. The meeting was organized by the appointment of B. W. Green, chair-

man, and John Brodhead, secretary.   Several appropriate and spirited addresses were delivered, in which
the sad occurrences of the afternoon were portrayed
in lively colours.   The speakers were E. M. Spencer,
Dr. John H. Gihon, General P. S. Smith, Col. C. G.
Childs, E. D. Tarr, T. R. Newbold, and Wm. D.
Baker.   The following resolutions were presented and
unanimously adopted:—

"*Resolved*, That the native American party of the city and
county of Philadelphia, attend *en masse* the bodies of those
martyrs of republicanism who were slain on Monday, the 6th
inst., in the district of Kensington, by a band of savage foreigners, to their last resting place, the grave.

"*Resolved*, That a committee of ten be appointed to make
arrangements with the families of the deceased, for the inter-
ments of the dead.

"*Resolved*, That a committee of three be appointed to inquire
into the circumstances of the families of the deceased.

"*Resolved*, That a reward of $1000 be offered by the Ameri-
can Republican party of the city and county, for the detection
of the perpetrators of the murders of the 6th inst., in addition
to the reward offered by the City and Commonwealth.

"On motion, *Resolved*, That the above resolutions be published in all the daily papers of this city.

"Committee to inquire into the necessities of the bereaved
families—John S. Germon, John Perry, John D. Fox.

"Committee for funeral—Col. C. G. Childs, E. D. Tarr, E.
W. Spencer, W. W. Hinckle, S. R. Kramer, Joshua Bethell,
Charles Warnock, John Brodhead.

"Committee on reward—T. R. Newbold, Wm. D. Baker, and
Thomas D. Grover."

Whilst this meeting was being conducted at the
Assembly Buildings, a scene of a different character
was being enacted in Kensington.   The news of the

6

outrage in the afternoon having spread through the
city, the most intense excitement and amazement
prevailed. Few could at first believe that such unprovoked and dreadful atrocities had been committed.
But as conviction was forced upon them, they were
bewildered; and as evening approached, many thousands of persons were hurrying towards the scenes of
violence, literally crowding the streets leading in that
direction.

CHAPTER VIII.

Vicinity of the Riots—Ruffians in the market-house—Bonfire—The crowd in Second street attacked by persons concealed in the houses —Retaliation—The female seminary—More murders—A man's thumb found in Perry street—Excitement increasing—Tone of the daily papers—Facts destined eventually to be known, and their influence felt.

FROM about seven o'clock on Monday afternoon, until after eight in the evening, the most profound silence prevailed in the immediate vicinity of the riots. About eight o'clock, the writer of this, in company with a friend, traversed the whole neighbourhood without meeting over a half-dozen individuals in the streets, within two squares of the scene of the afternoon's outrage. As they passed the market-house, however, they observed that a number of persons held it in possession, who it was afterwards ascertained were Irishmen, armed for further violence. At this time a large crowd had collected at the corner of Second and Franklin streets, which extended more than half a mile down Second street, and was momentarily receiving additions from the city. A short time after eight o'clock a large bonfire was kindled in Franklin street above Second, mostly by half-grown boys, which was kept burning for more than two hours by the constant heaping on of barrels and other fuel. The fire lighted up the whole neighbourhood, aud served in no

(63)

slight degree to increase the terrible excitement which pervaded the crowd. The light was seen at a great distance and created much alarm. At about ten o'clock, the crowd began to proceed gradually further up Second street; but when about half way between Franklin and Phœnix streets, a shower of brickbats and paving stones was poured down upon them from the roofs and windows of several houses. This sudden and unexpected attack caused a fearful rush down the street; but a number of persons soon rallied, and desperately assailed several houses from which this renewed outrage was perpetrated, and in an almost incredibly short space of time, completely demolished the doors and windows, and put to flight from the rear all their inmates. The exasperated crowd now moved up Second street, and when near the corner of Phœnix street, a number of fire-arms were discharged from a building formerly employed as a female seminary, by the Sisters of Charity belonging to the Catholic church, situated on the south-east corner of Phœnix and Second streets. This fire proved frightfully destructive. A young gentleman of much promise, Mr. John W. Wright, the son of Mr. Archibald Wright, commission merchant on Vine street wharf, was shot through the head and instantly killed; and several others were dreadfully wounded. One of these, Mr. Nathan D. Ramsey, lingered in extreme pain, until Wednesday evening, May 28th, when he died. Neither of these gentlemen were participating in any way with the disturbances, but were merely there as silent spectators of transpiring events. The intensely excited crowd now rushed toward the seminary, tore down and fired the fence, and assailed the building, but were prevented from doing further injury by the shots which continued to be poured in upon them. These shots came as well from the houses in the vicinity as from the seminary itself, all of which were in turn assailed by brickbats and paving stones. This state of things continued until near midnight, when the crowd dispersed, and order and quiet were once more restored.

Early on Tuesday morning the thumb of a man, with a large portion of the sinew attached, was found in a yard in Perry street, in the rear of the female seminary. It had been torn off by the bursting of a gun, on the night previous, and blown over the roof of a house to the place where it was discovered. The broken fragments of a gun-stock were also found in the vicinity. This thumb was afterwards ascertained to have belonged to an Irish Catholic, residing in Lombard street near Schuylkill Sixth, about three miles from where this well merited accident happened him; and the probability is, that he had gone all that distance from home to participate in the outrages for which he paid so dearly. He was subsequently arrested at the Pennsylvania Hospital, where he had been conveyed by his friends. His accident led also to the detection of two other participants in the riot. Blood was traced from where the gun exploded to the back door of a house in the vicinity of Second and Master streets. Mr. Albert Alberger, of Southwark, and two other gentlemen, upon learning this fact, procured

6*

a warrant, entered the house, and traced the blood
into the second story front room. Here they found
two men, named John O'Connor and Owen Daily,
whom they arrested and conveyed to Alderman
Boileau's office, where they were held to bail in the
sum of $1000 each to answer the charge of riot. In
the same room in which these men were arrested was
a loaded gun and some bloody sheets and pillow
cases. The man who lost his thumb had hastened
to this place previous to his having been taken to the
hospital.

The excitement throughout the city and county
during Tuesday morning was intense. Crowds of
people were assembled about the corners of the streets
and other public places, conversing of the outrages
of the previous day and evening, and business of every
description was almost entirely suspended. In Kensington, especially, the excitement was of the most
alarming character. Persons there boldly took sides
in dispute with either party engaged in the disturbances; and while the friends of the American party
expressed their utter indignation at the outrages which
had been perpetrated, some of the Irish Catholics
boasted of the manner in which the natives had been
beaten off, and of how much more severely they would
be beaten, should they attempt again to appear upon
the ground for a similar purpose.

At the offices of the daily papers in the city, an interest was observed rarely witnessed on any occasion.
Crowds of men and boys were gathered together,

eagerly awaiting new arrivals of information from the riotous district. The "Native American" and "Sun" issued extras, through the day, and so great was the rush after them, that the swiftest power presses upon which they were printed, could not supply one-half the demand. The prevalent feeling was in behalf of the Americans, and many who but the day before were arrayed in hostility against their cause, now came out boldly and zealously in its defence and advocacy.

Several of the party presses endeavoured to turn the current of public opinion by unfair statements of the outrageous occurrences. Not only perverted statements, but the most bare-faced and unblushing falsehoods were published and despatched to distant parts of the country. It was the policy and interest of their publishers to suppress the truth, and this they spared no means to effect. Hence they laboured to give the impression that the Americans were the real offenders, and their sympathies were all expended upon the riotous murderers, whose rights, it was maintained, were invaded, and their liberty of conscience assailed. But all this would not answer. The facts stood out before the populace in bold relief! *American citizens had been shot down in the public streets by foreign ruffians, for exercising privileges guarantied to them by the constitution under which they lived!!* A more violent outrage had never been committed. Nothing was more palpable than this. And though the press might deceive the public at a distance, it was impossible to conceal the truth from the immediate citizens, or to suppress the indignation, which, though for a time it was somewhat smothered, was destined in after years to be exhibited in a manner which was then but little anticipated.

CHAPTER IX.

Great Meeting in the State-House Yard—The speakers—Resolutions adopted—Adjournment to Kensington—No precautions taken by the authorities to prevent new Outrages—Unsuccessful attempt to organize the meeting—Another murderous assault by concealed Irishmen—Hibernia Hose-Carriage destroyed—The killed and wounded —John Taggart, an Irish rioter, captured and beaten.

ABOUT eleven o'clock on the morning of Tuesday, May 7th, a call appeared in the extras of the "*Native American*" and "*Sun*" newspapers, as well as in hand-bills on the corners of a few of the streets, for American citizens to assemble in mass meeting, at three and a half o'clock, P. M., in the State-House Yard. Long before the time named the people assembled in immense numbers, and at the opening of the meeting at least six thousand persons were assembled. The following officers were elected :

President—T. R. Newbold.

Vice Presidents—A. De Kalb Tarr, R. W. Green, John H. Gihon, John D. Fox, Thomas Taylor, Thomas D. Grover, John S. Warner.

Secretaries—James L. Gihon, A. R. Peale, Lewis C. Levin.

The meeting, thus organized, was briefly addressed by Mr. Newbold, who was followed in a speech of greater length, by Jas. C. Vandyke, Esq. The other speakers were Messrs. Wm. Hollingshead, John H.

(69)

Gihon, John Perry, and Col. C. J.,Jack. They seve-
rally alluded in mild, though positive terms, to the
outrages of the preceding day, and urged the assembly
to recompense the wrongs that had been done, not by
unlawful retaliation, but by bringing the offenders and
murderers to justice, and by the maintenance of the
American principles at the ballot-box at future elections. They were urged to bear as patiently as possible their injuries, and by all means, to act with that
regard for law, peace, and order, which should ever
characterize American citizens. These addresses in
all occupied about thirty minutes, when the subjoined
resolutions were offered by Mr. John Perry, with a few
appropriate remarks, and adopted unanimously:

"Whereas, a gross and atrocious outrage has been perpetrated in the district of Kensington, by which a meeting of
American citizens, assembled for the purpose of deliberating
on the affairs of our country, was disturbed and broken up, and
the lives of citizens wantonly and murderously sacrificed by a
band of ruffians firing into the crowd from places of concealment:

"We, the native American citizens of the city and county of
Philadelphia, in town meeting assembled, do hereby present
to our fellow citizens of all shades and distinctions of party,
the following resolutions:

"Resolved, That it is alike the right and the duty of all citizens peacefully to assemble for the purpose of expressing their
sentiments on the principles and actions by which our nation
should be governed.

"Resolved, That the interference with such assemblages by
others not participating in them, is an infraction of the rights
guarantied to us by the constitution and laws of our country.

"Resolved, That the recent outrage in Kensington, by which
a meeting was disturbed and broken up, and the lives of citi-

zens sacrificed, is an infraction of those rights which meets with the abhorrence of this meeting.

"*Resolved*, That whilst as men and Americans we are determined at all and every hazard to resist unto the death every infraction of our rights, we are determined that we will not be led by provocation to retaliate on the rights of others.

"*Resolved*, That the proceedings of a portion of the Irish inhabitants of the district of Kensington, on Monday afternoon, is the surest evidence that can be given, that our views on the Naturalization Laws are correct, and that foreigners, in the short space of five years, are incapable of entering into the spirit of our institutions.

"*Resolved*, That we consider the Bible in the Public Schools as necessary for a faithful course of instruction therein, and we are determined to maintain it there, in despite of the efforts of naturalized and unnaturalized foreigners, to eject it therefrom.

"*Resolved*, That this meeting believes that the recently successful efforts of the friends of the Bible, in the district of Kensington, was the inciting cause which resulted in the murderous scenes of the 6th inst.

"*Resolved*, That we approve of the proceedings of the meeting held at the Assembly Buildings last evening, by which a committee was appointed to make suitable preparations for the interment of the first martyr in the cause of civil and religious freedom among us, and that we recommend that the friends of our cause shall attend the funeral in a body.

"*Resolved*, That we also approve of the resolution passed at the same meeting, by which a reward of One Thousand Dollars is offered for the apprehension and conviction of the murderers.

"*Resolved*, That a collection be taken up for the benefit of widows, mothers, or children of the murdered."

A resolution was then offered, that when the meeting adjourned it should adjourn to meet in Kensington, on the following Thursday, but was lost. Another, proposing that the meeting should adjourn to assemble in Kensington on the following day, met with a similar fate. The officers of the meeting, and most of the speakers, advocated these resolutions, but other counsels prevailed. There were present those who insisted upon continuing the meeting in Kensington, and through their instrumentality it was

"*Resolved*, That the convention adjourn to meet at the corner of Second and Master streets."

This resolution, though protested against by the officers and others, was carried with loud and repeated cheering. The meeting then adjourned; but a portion formed in procession, and headed by Col. C. J. Jack, proceeded to the scene of the former day's riots. It is probable that this movement would not have been made, had not a report been extensively circulated, that the military had been called out by General Cadwalader, and that his brigade would be in Kensington to preserve the peace of the district, and protect the citizens against further violence. That no such precaution was taken by the sheriff was subsequently a source of the deepest regret. There was abundant reason to anticipate another outrageous breach of the peace, and an efficient officer would have had upon the spot either a civil or military force sufficiently large to prevent such a catastrophe.

The procession reached Master street about five o'clock, and preparations were commenced for conducting the business of the meeting on the open space between the market-house and the row of buildings from which the firing took place on the previous day.

But while in the act of raising their flag, the American party was again fired at from the direction of the Hibernia Hose-House. A rush was then made towards the house, when a volley of musketry was poured into the meeting. John Wesley Rhinedollar, a young man, was shot through the back and killed on the spot, and at least a half dozen others were wounded. Among these was a Mr. Lee, Peter Albright, and John Brodhead. Neither of these were seriously hurt. In a moment the hose-house was torn open by the infuriated crowd, the carriage taken out in the midst of a continuous discharge of fire-arms, and dragged away and destroyed. A destructive fire was now kept up without intermission, from the houses adjoining and in the rear of the hose-house, from persons entirely concealed from view. So great caution had been taken to guard against exposure, that it was no easy matter to determine from what direction the pieces were discharged. In a short time about thirty of the Americans were more or less injured. Several were dreadfully wounded. Mr. A. R. Peale was shot in the left arm, and the injured arm was subsequently amputated. Mr. George Young received a wound in the breast and fell weltering in his blood. The ball entered his left breast, passed through the lung, and escaped through his back below the shoulder.

This deadly, destructive, and unexpected assault again drove the Americans from the ground, and the Irish continued to discharge their guns at all who remained near enough to be injured by their fire. An Irishman, named John Taggart, was observed to be

7

especially active. He occupied a position in an alley,
where he would load his gun, then venture to the end
of the alley, take deliberate aim at whomsoever he saw
within his reach, and fire; and several times his shots
were known to take effect. At length he aimed his
piece at an old man, pulled the trigger and missed fire,
when his intended victim sprang forward, seized him
by the throat, and receiving assistance from the
crowd, secured him and carried him to the office of
Alderman Boileau. On his way thither the outraged
multitude fell upon him and beat him in a shocking
manner. He was examined and committed; but while
being taken to prison, was fallen upon by the crowd,
who placed a rope around his neck, and would have
hung him to the nearest post but for the interposition
of some of the more humane of the people. He was,
however, dragged along the pavement and again
severely beaten. Having thus expended their fury,
the crowd left him apparently dead, lying upon one
of the stalls in the market-house in Second street,
below Poplar. Thousands of persons gazed upon him,
and all supposed life to be extinct. From this place
he was taken to the Northern Liberties lock-up, where
he soon revived, was placed in the hands of a physi-
cian, and his wounds properly dressed. He subsequently recovered. The gun taken from this man
was loaded ten fingers deep with powder and slugs.

Until after six o'clock the Irishmen had the ascen-
dency. The Americans, amazed at the atrocity and
suddenness of the assault, and unarmed and helpless,
were standing about in groups, undecided as to their

future action. About this time a circumstance occurred
which turned the tide of affairs, and resulted in driving the murderous assailants from their places of
security.   Their triumph was of short duration, and
came nigh being purchased at a dreadful cost. They,
however, escaped the punishment which their atrocious
conduct so richly merited.

CHAPTER X.

A desperate battle—Buildings fired—Arrival of the Military—Moro murders—Renewal of disturbances—Spirit of retaliation—Irish rioters alarmed—American flags displayed from dwellings—St. Michael's Church set on fire—Priest Donahue—The Female Seminary destroyed—Dwellings and stores sacked and burned—Civil authorities at length aroused—Martial law.

ABOUT half-past six o'clock, some twenty of the Americans who had been driven off, returned to the scene of action, armed with muskets and rifles. This small party took a station immediately in front of the buildings occupied by the Irish assailants, on the open space where their friends had been shot, and opened a brisk fire upon their enemies, over whom, in a very short time, they obtained a complete victory. The bravery of the Americans here presented a remarkably striking contrast to the cowardice of their Irish foes. For while the latter, far superior in numbers, fired from places of concealment, the former stood boldly out in the open space, entirely exposed and unprotected. Soon after the fire was returned upon them, the Irish began to give way in evident alarm,—the building adjoining the hose-house was fired,—and none of them dared to expose themselves sufficiently to attempt to extinguish the flames, which spread with astonishing rapidity in a very brief space of time, until every house almost from which a gun had

(76)

been discharged, was enveloped in the devouring element. Their occupants precipitately fled from the rear of their burning buildings, and were about falling into the hands of the conquerors, when the sound of the military was heard approaching, who in a few moments took possession of the entire ground, and arrested all further hostile proceedings. This timely arrival of the troops, under command of General Cadwalader, was a fortunate circumstance for the original aggressors; for had they not reached the scene until half an hour later, in all probability those miserable men would have fallen victims to the fury which their own audacity and ferocity had aroused. Before the military approached, the torn and soiled flag which had been trampled upon and trailed in the dust, had again been elevated, and was floating near the spot where Shiffler, Rhinedollar, and others had fallen in their efforts to protect it. No attempt was made for some time to arrest the flames, which raged for several hours, and were not extinguished till at least fifty houses, including the Hibernia Hose-House, were entirely consumed.

Before the Irish were defeated in this last rencontre, a number of American citizens were added to the already long list of killed and wounded. Mr. Lewis Greble and Mr. Stillwell were shot dead. Mr. Joseph Coxe was mortally wounded, and died on the 23d of May. Mr. Lescher received a wound in the breast, which eventually occasioned his death. Matthew Hammitt died of a wound he received. Messrs. Wright, B. Ardis, Keyser, Thomas Fauston, William Hillman, a lad named Smith, and others, received

7 *

wounds, none of which proved fatal. In all, it was ascertained that eight persons were killed, and about forty others wounded. Several Irishmen were wounded, and one killed; though the full extent of the damage received by them was never learned. The market-house took fire from the burning buildings, and was destroyed.

Military companies having been dispersed through different parts of the riotous district, peace was again restored, and at 12 o'clock, all was again quiet. The fire at this time began to subside, and before daylight on Wednesday morning, had ceased burning. The entire row of houses from Jefferson to Master street, in Cadwalader street, and several others in Master street, were destroyed.

Early on Wednesday morning, May 8th, crowds again began to collect in the neighbourhood of the disturbances; but no hew outbreaks occurred until about 12 o'clock. By this time it was ascertained by the turbulent and reckless of those who were disposed to take side with the Americans, but who in fact were not members of that party, that the military, which still remained on duty, had received no authority to act decisively, and that it had been supposed that their presence alone was all that was necessary to prevent any further outrages. The folly of this supposition was soon made apparent. The mob now began to burn with a spirit of revenge against the Irish Catholics. A disposition to retaliate seemed to supersede every other feeling, and hence a few desperate fellows, among whom were some Irish Protest

ants, were determined to pursue the Catholics. They
no sooner learned that nothing was to be feared from
the presence of the military, than they commenced a
work of destruction, which the reflecting of all parties
most sincerely deplored. About 12 o'clock, they set
fire to a handsome brick dwelling-house, at the corner
of Jefferson and Washington streets, which, together
with an adjoining building, was consumed. Threats
were made that all the dwellings of the Irish Catholics
would be destroyed, and the utmost consternation pervaded that portion of the population. Small American
flags, and coloured rags, of every description, sewn
together to represent such flags, were hastily prepared
and hung from the windows of hundreds of houses in
the vicinity, to designate the residence of those favourable to the Americans, and to save them from the fury
of the rabble. The most, however, who exposed these
flags, were in fact, Irish Catholics, opposed to the
American cause, and many of them abettors, if not
actual participators, in the outrages that had been
committed. At three o'clock, the Catholic church
(St. Michael's) in Second street, between Master and
Jefferson streets, was fired. In a short time the entire
building was in flames, which communicated with the
priest's residence on the north, and a building on the
south, all of which were burned to the ground. The
priest, Donahue, had but a short time previous left
the premises in a cab. A loaded musket was found in
his house, before it was burned, and the barrels of
several guns were discovered in the ruins of the church.
On the preceding Sunday, this man had delivered a

discourse well calculated to inflame the passions of his ignorant hearers, and to produce the shocking scenes described.

Persons residing in the neighbourhood of the church testify, that during the early part of the riots, armed men were continually seen entering and leaving the building. Soon after the meeting-house was fired, the mob entered the female seminary at the south-east corner of Phœnix and Second streets, and having set it on fire, they deliberately proceeded to the grocery store on the opposite corner, kept by a man named Corr, who it was said had furnished the Catholics with ammunition, and broke in the windows and doors, and turned the contents of the house into the street. The seminary was destroyed. The residence of Patrick Clark, at the corner of Fourth and Master streets, and that of his brother, Hugh Clark, the police magistrate of the district, were next assailed, and their contents destroyed and thrown into the street.   The military stood looking on, silent and inactive witnesses of most of these scenes of violence and destruction. Several other houses were attacked, and considerable damage done to them, in consequence of reports having been circulated, and pretty satisfactorily proven, that their occupants had rendered assistance to the persons who had fired upon the American meetings.   During the progress of these events, many of the Irish Catholics removed the contents of their houses, and with their families left the neighbourhood. The accounts, however, given by some of the papers, of the extreme sufferings to which these were afterwards exposed in the woods, as well as the burning to death of women and children in the flames of the buildings that were consumed, were without any foundation in truth.

Having accomplished all the mischief they deemed desirable, in Kensington, the mob, or a very small part of it, proceeded to the city, and between eight and nine o'clock in the evening gathered about St. Augustine church, situate in Fourth street, below Vine. Here they were met by the mayor, who attempted to address them, which he did in a manner calculated to accomplish no possible good. A report had been circulated that the church was filled with armed Catholics, which report, those composing the mob were assured was unfounded; and they were virtually informed that the troop of horse which surrounded the building, had no power to do them injury. These assurances were by no means calculated to restrain their fury. They entered the church and set it on fire, and at ten o'clock it was completely enveloped in flames, which did not cease burning until everything was destroyed but the walls. The dwelling of Dr. Moriarty at the rear of the church was entered, and with all its contents was burned. Here the fury of the misguided men, or rather boys, for the most who perpetrated these outrages were minors, seemed expended, and they were content with the destruction they had effected.

Affairs having arrived at this crisis, the civil authorities became suddenly awake to a sense of their duty, and exceedingly active in its prosecution.

Reinforcements were added to the military, until
soldiers enough were in service to resist the encroachments of a foreign nation, had one invaded our shores.
Major General Patterson, supposing that the brigade
under General Cadwalader's command was insufficient
to keep in check the mere handful of men who were
actually engaged in the disturbances, called out the
whole division and placed himself at its head. The
governor also made his appearance in the city, and
was followed by several companies of infantry and
cavalry from the country, who, for all they were
needed here, had far better have remained at home.
The crew of the United States steamship Princeton,
which alone could have restored the peace, or kept it
from being broken, had they early been called out,
were in service. A large police force was also put
on duty, embracing nearly all the citizens not belonging to the military. Martial law was measurably
pronounced and enforced. The Catholic churches
were all placed under the protection of the military
and the police, and the streets leading to them were
in the evenings so guarded that citizens were not
permitted to pass through them. This state of affairs
continued for some days, and the city, county, and
state were subjected to immense expenditures of
money, which, by the timely interposition of the proper
officer, on Monday, the 6th of May, might all have
been saved, as well as the lives and property which
were sacrificed.

CHAPTER XI.

Description of the property destroyed, its probable value, and names
of the sufferers.

The following statements, which are clipped from
the "Dollar Newspaper" of May 15th, gives perhaps
as correct an account of the extent of damages to
property occasioned by the riots, as could possibly be
obtained:—

"The scene of the riots on Friday presented a spectacle of perfect desolation. Ruin lifted its wan and
haggard head through the blackened and yawning
walls on every side, while the emblem of mourning and
death hung from the muffled knocker and partly closed
shutter. It was a heart-sickening sight, the like of
which we hope we may never again look upon in this
or any other city; and next to this, the humiliating
display of the American bunting as a means of pro-
tecting the property of any class or sect of citizens
from the prejudices or destructive propensities of
another. Rows of houses for several squares round
the infected district, and in fact for some distance out
in the suburbs, have small tri-coloured flags pro-
truded from the windows—a sight mortifying and
humiliating to those who have been taught to believe
that our laws afford equal and efficient protection
to all.

" The amount of damage done to property was estimated by us on Friday, but we have reason to believe that we have underrated it. We found it impossible to arrive at a perfectly accurate computation of the loss, but we give the following as based upon the best possible conjecture, from the confused facts we have been enabled to collect.

" Mrs. Brady, whose house (a two-story brick), in Germantown road, above Master street, was attacked and riddled, and a portion of her furniture destroyed, suffered a loss of about $100.

" The brick house of John Lafferty, adjoining, was but slightly injured. Mr. Lafferty was not at home at the time of the attack upon his and Mrs. Brady's premises, and both were thus injured in their property, not because of any fault of their own, but because some of the persons pursued had fled up the alley which separates the two houses, and escaped by leaping the back fences.

" The damage to the property of Alderman Hugh Clark, corner of Fourth and Master streets, amounts to about $1000. This includes the destruction of the furniture of Patrick Clark, who occupied the corner house, and also his own furniture. It is difficult to estimate this damage accurately, as the alderman had a valuable library, which, together with papers, notes, receipts, accounts, &c., were all destroyed or stolen. The mother and brother of Alderman Clark resided in the house with him at the time of the riot, but they left before the mob attacked the premises. He is the police magistrate of the District of Kensington.

"Patrick Murray, who owned the large brick house at the corner of Germantown road and Jefferson street, which was sacked by the mob on Tuesday, must have lost about $4000 worth of property. He kept a grocery store on the premises, and had an extensive and valuable stock of groceries and flour, which was destroyed and scattered about the streets, or carried off by plunderers. Mr. Murray, we were informed, has been seriously affected in his mind in consequence of his losses.

"John Lavery, residing in Master street, below Germantown road, had his house and furniture, all he had in the world, destroyed. His loss is about $2000. He was the owner of the premises, a large and handsome brick house, with brick back-buildings. Mrs. Lavery was bewailing the breaking of the windows of the house by the rioters on Monday afternoon, little dreaming at that time that these outrages would be followed by the total destruction of the property.

"The two-story frame adjoining, owned by James Loy and occupied by Matthew Quin, was destroyed, and its value was about $150.

"On Cadwalader street, Bernard Sherry lost one frame and three brick houses, a quantity of goods, and all his furniture, except a single bed. His loss is about $3000.

"Patrick McKee's frame house, value about $400, was reduced to ashes. It was tenanted by Owen McCollough, who lost in furniture, materials, and manufactured goods, about $1000.

"One frame and two brick houses, owned by Thomas
8

Sheridan, and each occupied by tenants in his employ, and having his materials in their possession, for the purpose of manufacturing, were consumed, with all their contents. Loss about $2500.

" Michael Keeman, frame house and back building burned to ashes. Loss about $500.

" On Washington street, six three-story brick buildings, all tenanted, were destroyed. One was occupied by James Triner, and his loss, together with the value of the building, was at least $1500. Another was owned and occupied by James Munroe, formerly a brickmaker, and the loss is supposed to be about $2500. Wm. Steward owned and occupied another, with a back ingrain carpet manufactory, which, with the looms, wool, carpeting, &c., shared a similar fate. Loss not less than $4000, and probably much greater. John Mellon, in the same row, owned the house and lost all his furniture. Damage about $1500.

" Patrick Magee, who owned and occupied a large brick house at the corner of Washington and Jefferson streets, suffered a loss of about $1500. The circumstances attending the burning of this man's property were truly distressing. He was sick in bed at the time, and unable to move and effect his escape as the flames were crackling around him. He was in imminent danger of being consumed, when a neighbour, Mr. Munroe, hearing of his situation, rushed to his relief, and bore him to a place of safety. In a short time afterwards, his house was a heap of smoking ruins. The furniture and stock of this old man, which was destroyed, is not estimated in the above account of damage.

" Harmony court, running west from Cadwalader street, above Master, contained seven frame houses, three of which belonged to Mr. Charles Elliott, dry goods merchant, and four, on the other side of the way, to Mr. John Dougherty, tavern-keeper. They were all consumed—were worth about $400 each— making the loss about $2800. The tenants of these houses lost all their furniture and effects, valued at about $400 more.

" On Cadwalader street, second door from Jefferson, the house occupied by Hugh Develin was battered and damaged to a slight amount, but Mr. Develin lost property to the value of about $300. The house was owned by Messrs. Whitecar, of Spring Garden, one of whom was present when the attack was made, and by his remonstrances induced the mob to spare it.

" The loss to the Hibernia Hose Company, including carriage, hose, and hose-house, was not less than $1000. The carriage was but recently built, and a portion of the hose, 500 feet, was furnished by the commissioners of the district of Kensington.

" The market-house on Washington street, extending from Master to Jefferson streets, which caught from the conflagration of the dwellings in Cadwalader street, was originally built by a company, but was the property of the district of Kensington. The whole of this was destroyed—loss $3000 or $4000.

" John Heutzell's carpenter shop, in the rear of

Cadwalader street, entirely destroyed, and his house slightly injured.   Loss $400 or $500.

" Another building on Cadwalader street, owned by Mrs. Dobbins, and occupied by Ashton S. Hutchinson, as an ingrain carpet manufactory, with a dyehouse and a quantity of material—loss $1500.   Mr. Hutchinson, in his efforts to rescue some of his property from destruction, received several shots in his face and arm.   The wounds were not serious.

" The frame house of Mr. John Brown, in Cadwalader street, above the Hibernia hose-house, was destroyed.   Loss not ascertained.

" The two frame houses, at the corner of Master and Cadwalader streets, which were burned to the ground, belonged to John Carroll, and also two other frames adjoining.   Loss $1600.   The tenants lost all they had, say about $250.   It was in one of these houses that the $700 in silver was when it burned down, and but little of it having been recovered, this may be added to the other loss.

" The loss in the burning of the Catholic church of St. Michael, the parsonage house and furniture and ornaments, and the Sisters of Charity's seminary, is estimated at not less then $75,000.

" Of the five frame buildings on the right of the church, which were consumed, a three and two two-story frames belonged to Benjamin Hutchinson, Esq., who estimates his loss at $2500, and the other two belonged to Mr. Francis McCreedy and were valued at $1800.

" The loss to Mr. Joseph Corr, whose house at the

corner of Phœnix and Second streets, opposite the seminary, was sacked, is about $1500.

"The loss to Mr. McAleer, whose two large bricks, at the corner of Second and Master streets, were burned, is about $3000. The tenant of one of them, named Rice, lost about $600. A frame house back of this, owned by John Daley, which was burned, was valued at about $400.

"In estimating this destruction of property, we have not taken into account a vast amount of material in the houses occupied by workmen, nor of houses, the very sites of which have been obliterated; and we feel warranted in believing that the destruction of property amounts to much over what we have estimated.

"In addition to this we have to add the loss at St. Augustine's, and we will find that damage has been done to the county of Philadelphia, in a sum rising a quarter of a million of dollars; and this, beside the loss of life, and the deep moral stain which has been inflicted on the community. It appears that though this was a riot against the Catholics, yet the loss has also fallen heavily upon Protestant owners and tenants of property."

The same paper, in another article referring to these losses, furthermore remarked :—

"The direct loss to the city by the late riots, which has been estimated at not less than three hundred thousand dollars, has been far exceeded by loss from the lessened amount of business for the week. How large a sum has thus been kept from our city and been
8 *

sent to other cities, it would be next to impossible to estimate. Every man in business, however, can answer the question for himself, and it probably would not be excessive to assume that at least fifty per cent. of the more active description of trade has been cut off by the disorder and confusion that have prevailed. This will be found to amount to an enormous sum, if we run through the hundreds of wholesale and thousands of retail dealers of our city. The aggregate business of these in a week is probably several millions of dollars, the half of which has been driven away and lost to our citizens. This is an enormous sum, but, great as it is, the loss in the value of real estate from the withdrawal of capital and capitalists from our midst, will as greatly exceed the loss to trade as the latter does the loss by the actual burning and destruction of property. And the loss in character and moral influence, which will wear to our prejudice for years and years, far outweighs all other losses combined."

CHAPTER XII.

The Mayor calls a town meeting—Mass meeting of citizens of all
parties in Independence Square—Speech of Horace Binney—Resolutions adopted—The Sheriff directs the magistrates to call ward meetings—Citizens enrolled as voluntary patrols—Proclamation of the
Sheriff and Mayor—The Governor's proclamation—Opinion of the
Attorney-General—Presentment of the Grand Jury—Streets guarded
by the civil and military authorities—Card of the Catholic Bishop—
A clerical manœuvre to excite sympathy.

ON the morning of Thursday, May 9th, the following notice appeared in the daily newspapers, and was
posted through the streets:

"A town meeting of the citizens of the City and County of
Philadelphia, is invited to be held this morning, at 10
o'clock, at the Independence Square, to deliberate upon the present state of the public peace.   J. M. SCOTT, Mayor.
May 9, 1844."

In pursuance of this call, an immense multitude of
citizens assembled at the hour appointed, in the State-
House Yard.   It was supposed that full ten thousand
persons were present.   The meeting was called to
order by William M. Meredith; on whose motion
John M. Read was appointed Chairman, and Frederick
Fraley, Secretary.   The object of the meeting having
been briefly stated by the president, Horace Binney
came forward, and spoke as follows:

" FELLOW CITIZENS—In an emergency in which the lives and property of you all are threatened, you are convened for the purpose of adopting measures to remove and suppress the evil. It is necessary that you should act, and act promptly; and it is necessary to recollect that whatever has been done, has been done in scandalous violation of law. There can be no happiness, no security in this community, except in the maintenance of law. Whatever is to be done here, must be done to strengthen the hands of the law. Individually, I have not had twenty-five minutes to consider this question. My influence has been used to keep my own house in order. [Applause.] This has prevented me from reflecting on the subject, so as to offer remarks upon the course to be pursued. Excitement is not necessary. The fruits of excitement are already experienced. We have witnessed the horrible consequences of it. With the aid of a few friends, during the last fifteen minutes, a scheme has been agreed upon, the best that could be devised at the moment, to prevent the further progress of this enormous evil. I will say that we are under lawful organization to act in whatever scenes of trial our city may be exposed. We act under the authorities of the city, the county, and the state, and whatever is done, must be done by them, through them, and under them. But we must not forget that in scenes of violence where the authorities find it necessary to oppose force to force, they may err in the mode of discharging their duty. Still we ought to strengthen them by every means in our power, nor should their acts be too nicely weighed by fault finders, during exigencies, when time for reflection is scarcely allowed. They should receive the sympathy and support of you all. This is a body to carry into effect whatever is resolved upon. The citizens should give their aid in whatever manner the constituted authorities may deem best."

Mr. Binney then read and explained the following resolutions, which, having been seconded and appropriately commented upon by John K. Kane, were unanimously adopted:

"1. *Resolved*, by the citizens of the city and county of Philadelphia, that they will forthwith enrol and hold themselves in readiness to maintain the laws and protect the public peace, under the direction of the constituted authorities of the city, county, and state.

"2. *Resolved*, That the several aldermen and constables of the different wards be requested, as soon as possible, to take such measures as may be deemed necessary for the enrolment and organization of the citizens.

"3. *Resolved*, That the citizens be exhorted to abstain from assembling at or near the place of disorder and excitement, except under the direction of the proper authorities.

"4. *Resolved*, That the citizens of this city will, with the whole weight of their influence, means and strength, sustain the constituted authorities in the use of all lawful means for the preservation of the public peace, and will regard with the utmost favour the acts of the constituted authorities for that purpose, in the performance of their duty, under the guidance of the undoubted power of the law, that whatever degree of force is necessary to protect the lives and property of the citizens, by the constituted authorities, that force is lawful.

"5. *Resolved*, That the citizens be requested to meet in their several wards, at the places of holding ward elections, *this day*, at 2 o'clock, there to organize under the constituted authorities in support of peace and order.

"6. *Resolved*, That the sincere and hearty thanks of this meeting be, and they hereby are tendered to the several fire and hose-companies, who, by the promptitude with which they repaired to the scene of destruction, and by their perseverance, saved an incalculable amount of private property."

Gen. Adam Diller then offered the following preamble and resolution, which being adopted, the meeting, on motion of Josiah Randall, adjourned:

"Whereas, It is believed that a great portion of these rude assemblies is made up of young boys, who are incompetent of

foreseeing the evil consequences of such illegal acts, and it is
believed that parents and masters could prevent these youths
from attending the scene of riot,

"Therefore, *Resolved*, That the civil authorities be requested
to call, by proclamation, upon the heads of families and masters,
requesting them to keep their young men and boys at home
during the prevailing excitement."

The sheriff, on the morning of this same day, had
also issued the following notice :

"ALDERMEN, ATTEND !--The magistrates in the different
wards and townships of the city and county of Philadelphia,
are requested to convene the citizens of their respective wards,
this afternoon, at 4 o'clock, at the usual places of holding the
ward elections, to take measures to preserve the public peace.

May 9, 1844.   MORTON McMICHAEL, Sheriff."

In compliance with the foregoing suggestions, meetings were called in all the wards and townships of the
city and county, by the different aldermen, which were
accordingly held at the various ward-houses. At these
meetings salutary resolutions were adopted, and numerous citizens enrolled themselves as voluntary patrols,
to protect the city from further disturbance, and to
serve night and day, until quiet and peace were restored. About noon, too, the following proclamation
was posted in every part of the city and county :

"PROCLAMATION.—The sheriff and mayor, under the authority of the laws, and the recommendation of the citizens of the
city and county of Philadelphia, in town meeting assembled,
declare and proclaim, that all persons whomsoever, are forbid-
den to be or appear in any streets or places, in the city or
county, which are, or may be in the occupation of the civil
authorities, or of the militia, for the preservation of the lives
and property of the citizens. And the officers of the militia

are hereby authorized to declare what streets and places are thus occupied, and to employ such force of arms as may be necessary to compel obedience to this order. Fire-engines and hose-carriages are required not to enter such streets or places, without the permission of the civil or military authorities.

MORTON McMICHAEL, Sheriff.

J. M. Scott, Mayor of Philadelphia.

May 9th, 1844."

On the same day the governor of the commonwealth also issued a proclamation, which is here given :—

"PROCLAMATION OF THE GOVERNOR.

GENERAL ORDERS.

Head Quarters, May 9, 1844.

David R. Porter, Governor of the Commonwealth of Pennsylvania, and Commander-in-Chief, &c.—Orders as follows, to wit :—

Whereas, he has received information from the regularly constituted authorities, that large bodies of riotous persons have assembled in the city and county of Philadelphia, within the last two days, and manifested a disposition to persist in the same course of organized efforts to disturb the public peace, and to kill and slay the citizens of this commonwealth, to burn and destroy churches, houses, and other property belonging to the citizens, and that the usual means employed by the sheriff and mayor have thus far proved inadequate to check the turbulence and outrage of said riotous assemblages ; and whereas, he has also been informed that the lives of a number of persons have been sacrificed, and that numerous houses and churches have been burned and destroyed—he issues the following orders :—

First. It is ordered by the commander in chief that the sheriff of the county of Philadelphia, the mayor of the city, and all the magistrates, constables, and citizens, be directed and requested to co-operate for the preservation of the public peace, and the dispersion of the riotous assemblies above referred to.

Second. It is ordered by the commander-in-chief, that Major-General Patterson be directed to call into immediate service all the volunteer companies, belonging to the first division of the Pennsylvania militia, and so to order and distribute them, as well as all other volunteer companies who have been ordered to report themselves to him, as to suppress in the most effectual manner the assemblies referred to, and to disperse or procure the arrest of the persons engaged in the same.

Third. It is ordered by the commander-in-chief that, when called upon by the sheriff of the county, or mayor of the city, General Patterson shall adopt the necessary precautionary measures to clear and occupy, by an adequate portion of his force, any street, alley, or private property, to protect the same from riot, disturbance, or destruction; and that he employ, in any emergency, such a degree of force or resistance as shall be necessary to maintain the public peace and safety of unoffending individuals.

The commander-in-chief avails himself of this opportunity, of expressing his entire approbation of the measures adopted during this day by the sheriff, mayor, and major-general of the first division, for the preservation of the public peace, and the enforcement of the laws.

He also expresses his entire concurrence with the attorney general in his opinion this day addressed to the sheriff and mayor, on all the questions therein answered. He confidently hopes that all good citizens will promptly unite in the suppression of these disgraceful tumults, and in the maintenance of order and tranquillity. He at the same time does not hesitate to avow, that in his opinion the time has arrived for the most vigorous and energetic measures; and dreadful as may be the alternative, the last and most fatal resort to means destructive even of the lives of offenders, is far better than the continuance of such disgraceful outrages. Relying upon the patriotism of the citizen soldier, who is thus called upon in the hour of peril to protect the institutions of his country from assault, the commander-in-chief is confident that no soldier will under any circumstances fail to discharge his whole duty, and to preserve his own and his country's honour untarnished.

By order of the governor and commander-in-chief.

ADAM DILLER, Adjutant-General, P. M."

In order that no mistake should occur in regard to the nature and extent of their authority and power, the mayor and sheriff conjointly addressed a communication to the attorney-general, whose opinion on the subject in reply thereto, is also subjoined:

"THE OPINION OF THE ATTORNEY-GENERAL.

Attorney-General's Office, Philadelphia, May 9th, 1844.

GENTLEMEN—In compliance with your request of this morning, I most willingly state to you my opinion on the points submitted for my consideration.

The power to preserve the public peace, and to maintain the authority and observance of the laws, is undoubtedly, in the first instance, vested in the high sheriff of the county, and mayor of the city. All magistrates, subordinate officers, and citizens, are subject to the order and direction of one or the other of these functionaries, or both, as the emergency may require. If need be, the governor of the commonwealth may be called on to interpose, with the entire force of the state. The military is also subject to the requisition of these authorities, when proper cases for making the requisition, arise.

The question as to how much force may be employed to suppress riots, disorders, and breaches of the peace, is at all times one of great delicacy and responsibility; but it is one on which in critical conjunctures, no doubt whatever exists.

If a riotous body of men assemble with the avowed or manifest design of taking life, doing great bodily harm, or of firing buildings, or destroying property in which danger to life or personal safety may be involved, and they resist the legally constituted authorities, and persist in the prosecution of their design, it is perfectly clear that just as great a degree of force may be employed to disperse or arrest them, as is necessary to effect that object. If they take life, or threaten to do so with the means of executing their threat, their lives may unques-

9

tionably be taken, in the same manner as if they were open public enemies or pirates. The public streets, or even private property, may be occupied by the force employed in maintaining order, to the exclusion of every other object.

Of course, the emergency must be a clear one, and the order given by the proper officer recognised by the laws, as vested with the power, in order to justify this terrible appeal to the *last means* of preserving the public safety.

I know this power has been sometimes questioned, but without its possession, our government would be a mere shadow. It would profess to do what it is denied the power to do; and it would be, as it ought to be, held in utter contempt for its imbecility. The great principle of self-preservation lies at the foundation of our government; and on this principle, any degree of force is justifiable that is indispensably necessary.

I should, therefore, not hesitate an instant, to use all the force that was necessary to this end, against whomsoever may be found with arms in their hands, to take life, or with the manifest determination to burn down or destroy buildings, and trample on the laws.   Yours very respectfully,

                                        OVID F. JOHNSON.

To Morton McMichael, Esq., High Sheriff,
    John M. Scott, Esq., Mayor."

Agreeably to a suggestion of the county commissioners, the grand jury made a presentment to the court of quarter sessions, which was likewise published, and read as follows:

"PRESENTMENT.

To the Court of Quarter Sessions of the Peace of the city and county of Philadelphia, by the Grand Jury:—

The grand inquest respectfully present that their attention has been called by the county commissioners to the deplorable scenes of riot and mob violence, which have occurred within the last two days in the district of Kensington, involving the destruction of a vast amount of property for which large drafts may be made upon the county treasury.

The grand jury are sensible of the loss likely to accrue to the county by the destruction of property referred to, and whilst regretting the same, cannot withhold their opinion that the open violation of law and order, and contempt of the civil authorities manifested in Kensington, and subsequently in the city of Philadelphia, by the burning of the St. Augustine church, are much more to be deplored than any pecuniary loss consequent thereupon.

The grand jury would earnestly call to the attention of the court, the propriety of arousing the citizens generally to a sense of the necessity of their rallying to the support of the authorities, in restoring order and maintaining the supremacy of the law.

The grand jury will most cheerfully unite in any effort to accomplish these most desirable ends, in which every citizen desirous of restoring public order, and preserving the city and county from anarchy and bloodshed, should unhesitatingly lend his aid.

The grand jury submit to the consideration of the court, the letter of the county commissioners above referred to, and desire that it may be considered a part of the presentment.

The grand jury present, that to their knowledge lives have been lost in the riots to which this presentment refers, and whilst deeply sympathizing with the families and friends of the slain, and making all allowances for acts committed under the frenzy of excitement, they consider that sufficient time has elapsed for the abatement of such feelings, and that they are no excuses for the destruction of buildings erected for the worship of God.

Jno. M. Brown, Forem'n,	Wm. Loughlin,
Charles J. Ashmead,	Isaac Bedford,
Wm. Rovoudt,	Jacob H. Smith,
John Paisley,	Geo. W. Smick,

Alex. Austin,	Jos. J. Bishop,
Wm. Nassau, Jr.,	Jos. B. Linerd,
Geo. Follin,	R. W. Pomeroy,
Wm. H. French,	Benj. Mifflin,
John Kingston,	W. Wurtz,

Joseph Moore."

In accordance with the foregoing resolutions, suggestions, proclamations, and orders, the city was placed under the charge of the military, regular police, and volunteer aids, in sufficient numbers, not only to preserve its peace, but to resist successfully an invading army. All the streets, where any disturbances, or indications of disturbance, had taken place, were strongly guarded, and the Catholic churches, especially, were placed under the protection of the civil and military authorities. But notwithstanding all these precautions, these positive assurances that no further harm was intended or could be perpetrated, the Catholic Bishop had the bad taste to publish the following card:

"TO THE CATHOLICS OF THE CITY AND COUNTY OF PHILADELPHIA.

BELOVED CHILDREN—In the critical circumstances in which you are placed, I feel it my duty to suspend the exercise of public worship in the Catholic churches, which still remain, until it may be resumed with safety, and we can enjoy our constitutional right to worship God according to the dictates of our conscience. I earnestly conjure you to practise unalterable patience under the trials to which it has pleased Divine Providence to subject you, and remember that afflictions will serve to purify us and render us acceptable to God, through Jesus Christ, who patiently suffered the cross.

† FRANCIS PATRICK,

Bishop of Philadelphia.

Philadelphia, May 9th, 1844."

This card presents a rare specimen of barefaced insolence and hypocritical audacity. The bishop addresses his people, who he well knew were either the perpetrators or instigators of all the mischief that had been done, as having been most shockingly abused, and calls upon them to submit patiently and meekly, as did their Saviour, to the persecutions they had been and were still being compelled to endure for Christ's sake! He furthermore directs them to suspend the exercise of public worship until it could be resumed with *safety*, and consequently, on the following Sunday, all the Catholic churches were closed. Now, the bishop knew, as did every citizen, whether Catholic or Protestant, Jew or Infidel, foreigner or native, that the Catholics were just as safe on that day " to worship God according to the dictates of their consciences" as were the members of any other religious sect. No danger, whatever, was apprehended. Mischief enough had already been done, and there was no disposition to do more, unless it was on the part of the original aggressors, and they were the last to interfere with the worship of Catholics. The bishop seemed dissatisfied with the calm that had followed the destructive storm, and was evidently disposed to fan into a new flame the smouldering embers of the

9 *

late conflagration. The fires that the Catholic rioters
had kindled had scorched themselves—they had lost the
battle they had waged—the weapons they hurled had
rebounded to their own injury—and it was now a
cunning stroke of policy to avert the indignation they
had excited, and call forth the sympathies of those
unacquainted with the facts, to raise the hue and cry
of religious persecution and intolerance; and hence
their churches were closed and religious worship was
suspended. The cloven foot was plainly seen beneath
the garments of the body that owned it. It was less
a source of regret to the Catholics that churches had
been burned, than that they could not provoke, by
continued outrages, the burning of still more churches.

CHAPTER XIII.

ALLUSION has been made to the spirit of the newspaper press at the period when the foregoing events were transpiring. The daily "*Native American*" claimed to be the *organ* of the American party. Its columns exhibited a rather vacillating and temporizing policy, and lacked the vigour, energy, force, strength, and power the exigencies of the time demanded. It lived but a short period, and its demise was neither a source of gratification to the opponents, not of regret to the friends of the American cause. From its leading editorial of May 13th, the following paragraphs are taken:

"Who were the rioters by whom the arsons were committed? We have investigated this matter as far as our time and opportunities would permit, and we have no hesitation in saying, that two-thirds of them were minors, and the residue the very scum of the population. Any one who has witnessed the crowds of the former who "run," as it is termed, with some of the fire companies, can readily conjecture that in times like those through which we have passed, a crowd of ragamuffins can be gathered together, ripe for any scene where violence is promised. This gang of ruffians assumes the name of a popular party, and in that name commit outrages which any man of common sense can see at a glance policy alone, if no higher motive, would prevent any party committing. We believe most sincerely, on a full review of the whole affair, that if the chief civil magistrate of the county had on Monday discharged fearlessly and impartially his duty, no outbreak would have occurred, no lives have been lost. Had he gone as he was requested to do, to the ground, we do not believe a breach of the peace would have occurred. The men who committed the outrage then would have respected his presence, and the moral influence of that presence would, before blood was warmed by a taste or sight of it, have restrained the whole thing.

"In this view we are sustained, we believe, by almost the entire mass of the reflecting portion of the population. A lesson has been taught in our future elections to inquire further into the fitness of a man for such an office than his mere political affinities."

The "*Sun*" had also hoisted the American standard, and become an advocate and defender of the American republican movements. The editor, L. C. Levin, wielded a ready, fearless, and powerful pen. His leading editorial of the 11th May, was a vigorous article, of which we give a part:

"We have ever been, and always shall be, the stern

and uncompromising foes of riot, disorder, and Lynch
law, in all its variety of forms and phases, and have
ever denounced them, in all seasons, and in all cases,
through the columns of "The Sun;" when other
journals, now smirking in hypocritical softness, have
been the open and profligate champions of Lynch law,
by appeals to the most detestable passions of the vilest
herd that ever disgraced humanity. If we have any
influence over the conduct of a solitary human being
who has been injured, we say to him, redress your
wrongs by the laws or by the ballot-boxes—reserve
your energies to be concentrated in a legal and constitutional manner, and never let provocation, however
galling, tempt you into the commission of a wrong, in
retribution for an injury. Burn no churches, even if
your fathers were murdered before your eyes. Give
a more rational and effectual direction to your feelings, by making the ballot-box speak in tones of thunder against the aggravating wrongs you have endured.
Let reason guide your conduct, not passion. Give
your enemies no pretexts for putting you in the wrong,
when they themselves have been the aggressors. Respect their churches and their rights, and peaceably
exercise your elective franchise so as to obtain an
ample and sure award of damages for all your wrongs.
These are the *legal and proper remedies* which will
always make your enemies smart most bitterly.

"This brings us to consider the primary cause of
these fierce outbreaks, which had their origin in the
'Repeal Clubs,' and the inflammatory language of
their leaders. The fomentors and agitators of these

riots, are to be found in the hostile array of foreign factions, against American rights and institutions, which brought native Americans and this press in common with them, up to the work of *self-defence*. This has been our attitude from first to last, and we make the explanation to strip our adversaries of their artful devices to put us in the wrong, when *all the wrong* has been on their side—all the tumult—all the mob-violence and all the butchery. We say this, in justice to truth and not to exasperate our friends, who we hope will remain calm and tranquil, and do nothing unbecoming American citizens and pious Christians; but we do assert it before the most holy Father of mercies, that we are the wronged party, and that we stand like persecuted martyrs, defending our lives and liberties. It was not *until* the American flag had been trampled under foot, and a public meeting of free citizens dispersed by physical force, that the editor of this paper yielded *to the solicitations of the people*, to address the meeting in Kensington. The people had a right to expect that the public authorities would have protected them in the peaceful exercise of that constitutional right. How we were assailed and driven from the ground is known. Now we ask in all soberness and solemnity befitting the occasion, wherein the people who there assembled were in the wrong? At the meeting in the State-House Yard, we were not present, but no man will dare to question the right or decorum of the people on that occasion. It was quiet, orderly and *self-defensive*. But why was that and the other meeting odious to the foreign population? We ask this of the Repeal Clubs and their organs. Why, because *they* had fomented the passions of the Irish to madness. Because *they* had turned *traitors* to American principles, and prostituted the American press against American institutions. Nay, so far did they go in their invasions upon American rights, as to attempt *to silence* this press *by intimidation*, from speaking in behalf of American institutions! We were brow-beaten and threatened for espousing the cause of the Bible, when they succeeded in driving it from our schools. Here then was a critical and responsible position. We were required to surrender *the Liberty of the Press*, to the dictation of the Repeal Clubs. This was the first wrong done us, on which we stood *on the defensive.* Next we were required to surrender *the Liberty of Speech.* After that, we were required to surrender the right of public meeting."

In the same paper of the 13th of May, the editor used the following strong and emphatic language :

" The studied efforts made by those guilty of *commencing* the late disgraceful scenes of riot and outrage, to throw the censure of their authorship upon the Americans and Protestant Irish, are among the weapons which history shows us to be familiar with those who act under the influence of a ' Church and State' power. Sophistry, equivocation, duplicity and mental reservation are a few of the prominent elements that truth and republicanism have to encounter from leaders, who urge on an ignorant and deluded rabble to apply *physical force*, to strangle the rights of a free people, supplying them with 'the sinews of war,' and their counsel to mature and direct their plans.   We all know, because history has informed us, of the subtle policy of that power, which was always ready to plot and execute bloody persecutions, and when baffled in their views or repulsed in their attacks, to put on the meek face of suffering innocence, and give out to the world, that they were persecuted, proscribed, and living martyrs of others, because others had been roused to *self-defence* against their Guy Fawkes plots and infernal machinations.   History has painted these features in characters too bold and indelible ever to be mistaken or effaced.   The recent suspension of worship in the Catholic churches, even after the order of General Patterson, is one of those cunning affectations of persecution that have become too common to deceive any into a false sympathy for their pretended religious persecutions.

"Who ever interfered with their religion?   Certainly not those who contended for their own legal rights to the use of the Bible.   Is the burning of their churches to be adduced as evidence of such interference?   Are the mad outrages of a mob to be referred to those who contend for the Bible and the purity of the ballot-box?   What connexion can possibly exist between the murder of some score or two of Americans, by Catholic rifles, while quietly attending a public meeting, and *their* observance of religious rights, *after* the riot had been quelled by military force?   The Catholic Irish *commence* a bloody assault upon an American meeting, which lasts three days, and costly arms are found in the hands of men scarcely able to buy bread—arms sufficient to equip a small army, showing *deliberate* preparation for a murderous assault; and when the affray is ended, lo! the leaders of these deluded beings put on a sanctimonious air and close their churches! If the contest had commenced with the Americans, or Irish Protestants, their churches, on a rational presumption, would have been the first objects of hostility. But this was so far from being the fact, that some twenty Americans are barbarously murdered before the exasperation of a mob draws it to the crime, the horrid crime of church burning; proving clearly that the mob had lost all reason in their resentment, and acted without motive or object, other than what are common to all mobs, the work of ruthless destruction, directed against the most prominent and visible object of the murderous and assailing party.

"Splendid rifles, and warlike munitions, not appropriate to their condition, have been found in the possession of Irish Catholics of *the lowest grade* of poverty, clearly showing that the chief actors, or instigators in this bloody assault upon peaceable Americans, are yet *behind the scenes*, and that they are persons of wealth, thus clearly indicating the deep-laid schemes of the conspirators, by heads as clear as their hearts were black.

"Had the Americans been the aggressors, they would have gone armed to *the first* place of meeting. But we find they were utterly *defenceless*. None had

10

weapons at the first meeting of the Americans when
they were dispersed, and their flag trampled on!
Where were their weapons at the *second* meeting, when
attacked and shot down by the splendid rifles of *the
Irish Catholics?*   On the side of the Catholics, *elabo-
rate preparations* of a murderous nature were found to
have been made by the cowardly assassins.   It was
only at the third meeting, that the Americans thought
of arming in *self-defence*, and even then, *the intention*
was not carried into effect.   With the knowledge of all
these facts, and the admitted power of the priests over
their flocks—a power more formidable to them, than
governor, general, mayor, and sheriff combined—still
no priest appeared, to subdue the bitter and bloody
strife."

The most of the neutral papers were contented with
simply reporting the disturbances, without committing
themselves by the expression of decided opinions in
regard to their causes.   Some of them, in fact, kept a
close eye to their own interests, and trimmed their
sails and shifted their courses to suit the changing
winds and currents of popular feeling.   The "*Public
Ledger*," however, occasionally gave an excellent article, in which important truths and correct sentiments
were clearly stated and ably discussed.   A few of these
have obtained a place in these pages.   The "*Daily
Forum*" was the Whig penny paper of the day.   This
paper attributed the riots to the violence of the repeal
orators and their opponents, and to the religious animosities existing between Catholics and Protestants; but

its tone, though whining, was decidedly unfavourable to
the Americans.   Every possible excuse that sophistry
could command, was made for those who it could not
deny were the instigators and original actors in the
Kensington riots.   With the editor of this paper, the
disturbing of a quiet political meeting by foreigners;
the murder of American citizens in the streets; and
all the other outrages that were committed on the part
of the Irish Catholics, were matters of but trifling moment: while the holding of American meetings in
districts thickly inhabited by Irish; the routing of
these from their houses after their murderous assaults;
and the burning of Catholic churches, were offences of
the greatest magnitude. The " United States Gazette,"
also a Whig journal, overflowed with sympathy for the
poor creatures who had been driven from their homes,
and compelled to take shelter in the neighbouring
woods; though it had but little to bestow upon the
persons who had been wounded in the streets, or the
families of those who were mercilessly murdered. The
" Daily Chronicle" was a neutral paper, but laboured
with no little zeal to defend the sheriff from the charges
that were so freely made against him for his non-inter-
ference in the commencement of the riots.   This was
a difficult task; but the editors persevered in its performance with becoming talents and industry.

CHAPTER XIV.

THE "*Spirit of the Times*" was professedly a democratic paper, but it degenerated into a mere organ of the Irish Catholics, to whose prejudices it pandered without stint or measure. It had long been struggling against a disease that threatened its dissolution, and the outbreaks at Kensington opportunely happened to prolong a little while its sickly existence. It denounced the Americans in unmeasured terms—condemned them as the originators of the outrages that were committed—and defended and justified the opposite party. That party needed just such an organ, and they at once rallied around it, and saved it for a limited period from impending ruin. The subscriptions poured in rapidly, and the advertising columns received a corresponding increase of patronage. This work would be imperfect were we to neglect giving a few specimens of the spirit of this press. In the leader of the 9th of May, the following language was employed :—

" We are still in the midst of a scene of carnage and destruction that makes us, an American by birth, inclination, and education, blush for our people, and fear for the permanence of republican institutions. Can it

(112)

be possible that men who boast of their intelligence—
men who know the value of good laws, and the imposing necessity of yielding implicit obedience to them—
men who have been indoctrinated with Christian principles, and avow their every private and public action
subject to them, can it be possible that such men plead
the law of retaliation for injuries—like the untaught
savage set at defiance all moral, all legal, all Christian obligations—and bathing their hands in human
blood, send soul after soul unprepared into eternity, as
an atonement for a private and personal wrong? Can
it be possible that men dare thus to constitute themselves judges, juries, and executioners in their own
case, with such words as liberty and justice, God and
their country, still lingering upon their lips? It is
fearful to think so.

"Not only have those who have participated in
these murderous riots no reasonable apology for their
iniquitous conduct, but the designing or the misled
spirits who urged them on have still less. Look at the
mass meeting held at the State-House Yard on Tuesday at noon. They met, and properly too, to condole
with the bereaved, and to utter their determination to
maintain their unalienable rights. But alas! was there
no gentle being present to press on the multitude the
wisdom, the importance of forbearance? Was there
no eloquent tongue present to point to the court-house
and the administrators of justice there seated, and
designate them as the proper place and persons for the
retribution of every public wrong? Was there present
no minister of divine things to teach the excited mass

10 *

HISTORY OF THE AMERICAN PARTY.

to abstain from violence, to imitate the sublime example of him who was not only 'a man of sorrows and acquainted with grief,' but blessed the peace-maker, and enjoined upon us to leave vengeance to One who never erred in his righteous dispensations?

"We conscientiously believe that had not that meeting been held, or had not resolved to adjourn in a body to Kensington, and by its presence stirred up the dormant ill-feeling of the belligerents on both sides, there would have been no riot, no bloodshed, on that lamentable night. What, then, have they to answer for who, in their blindness, counselled such unfortunate conduct? What have they to answer for, who, identifying in inflammatory speeches Christianity itself with anything but forbearance, prepared all who listened for acts of violence? What have they to answer for who, on such an occasion and knowing the dreadful consequences, persisted in mingling religion with politics, until many dreamed that in committing homicide they would be doing good service to 'God and their country?' We respect every man's opinion, we respect those who are sincere even in error, but we protest again and again against this unholy alliance, and be they clergymen or laymen, those who by their counsel induced the meeting to adjourn to Kensington, first exasperating its members with pictures of religious intolerence, *on their heads be the murders of Tuesday night!*"

On Monday, May 13th, the same writer indulged in the following pathetic strain, which, had it contained

more truth, would have been as creditable to the heart
as it was to the head of its author. He possessed a
lively imagination, and drew his pictures with a pencil
most elaborately coloured. We give but a few paragraphs of a very lengthy editorial:

"All was quiet in our city yesterday. It was a
strange thing, however, to see the military promenad-
ing our streets on the Sabbath, but still stranger to
feel that their presence was necessary to the maintenance of the public peace! Into all the churches,
as the chiming bells pealed out their solemn tones,
poured crowd after crowd of citizens to give thanks,
perhaps, to the Deity for their safety. Into *all* the
churches we should have said, *excepting*—the Roman
Catholic. They stood desolate, silent, and un-
tenanted. In obedience to the orders of the bishop
they were not opened for public worship. The solitary tread of the sentinel, or the clank of the musket,
was the only sound that disturbed *their* solitary
repose.

"And this was a Sabbath picture of the 'City of
Brotherly Love!' This was a picture of the 'Quaker'
city! Could William Penn have risen from his grave
and looked at such a scene; could he have gazed on
the bristling bayonets that offended the quiet eye in
almost every direction; could he have been told that
this pomp and panoply of war were necessary to secure
the liberty of religious opinion; that here, on this
very spot where he had planted the Christian banner,
which he had made the asylum of the persecuted for

opinion's sake, and had peculiarly consecrated to
religious freedom; could he have been told that *here*
all this exhibition of military force was required simply
to enable men to exercise one of the inalienable privileges of humanity, to worship God according to the
dictates of their own consciences, what that great and
good man would have said we leave the reader to
imagine. He could not have credited the evidence
of his senses. He could not have believed his descend-
ants so monstrously degenerated. He could not have
dreamed for a moment that the people of his own
Christian city would ever practise that bigoted
intolerance to escape from which he himself abandoned
his country, his kindred and his home, and as an un-
dying monument of his abhorrence of which he founded
the community in which we live.

"We grow sick of such unmitigated hypocrisy.
We shudder when we think that all these hideous outrages were perpetrated in the name of a God whose
eye, as he beholds them, pierces through the thin disguise that envelopes their gross turpitude, and reads
the impious hearts of those who thus mock at his infinite
wisdom and justice!

"Look at the crumbled ruins of Kensington, and
at the blackened bones of the slaughtered that lie
mixed up with the still smoking cinders. Look at
what is left of the frowning walls of St. Augustine, upon
one of which, though begrimed by smoke, are still
visible the ominous words 'HE SEES ALL,' as if addressed to the smitten conscience of every beholder.
Look at the famishing ones driven forth by the

spoilers, and now wandering houseless and homeless, suffering for their faith. Look at the Catholic clergy walking our streets in disguise, fearful of recognition. Look at the vultures tearing open the graves of the dead at St. Michael's, or breaking the silent tomb-stones in demoniac rage. Look at these things, and if you have the courage, say—all this was done in the Republic of America! this was done by men who boasted that they were natives of the ' Land of Liberty!' This was done in the name of the Bible! This was done to glorify the flag of the union! Say this if ye dare, all who love human freedom! Say this if ye dare, all who can truly boast of being not Americans by *birth* only, but Americans by nature! Say this if ye dare, all who are really Christians !"

Now, all this is very pretty. It was intended for a special purpose,—to delude still more an already deluded people,—and to prop up a sinking cause and give new life to a dying paper. Let us carefully, though hastily, glance over this subject. The " Times" (and other prints used similar language) preaches eloquently about the sufferings of the poor Catholics, who were driven from their homes and not permitted to visit their churches. Let us admit these statements to be true, and endeavour to ascertain the origin of the sufferings for which so much sympathy is expressed. On Friday night, May 3d, an Irish mob violently AS-SAULTED, BROKE UP, and DISPERSED a meeting of respectable American citizens, lawfully convened to

express their political sentiments. No attempt was
made to resist their assailants, much less resort to
violence in retaliation. On the following Monday,
however, another attempt was made to hold the meeting, when thousands of peaceable citizens assembled,
and in open daylight. In the mean time, their
former assailants had been *secretly* and *savagely* pre-
paring themselves with fire-arms and ammunition in
great abundance, "venting threats of slaughter and
destruction" upon the Americans. And in the very
midst of the meeting, than which a more orderly and
peaceable one was never held, before a solitary excep-
tionable sentence had been uttered, and ere *any provocation* had been given; out of windows, alleys, from
behind walls and fences, and through holes bored in
the houses, volley after volley of stones and musketry
were fired into a defenceless collection of at least two
thousand persons, dealing death and destruction on
every side. And a young man, whose *only offence* was
clinging to the flag of his country, was shot through
the heart, and died! Never, since God made this
world, was there a more brutal outrage perpetrated
upon its fair surface! Never was there an act of
violence committed for which there can be found less
excuse! Never was there a time when the public press
had more cause to cry aloud in tones of thunder in
defence of right, and in condemnation of aggression
and barbarity! But faint indeed was the voice which
many portions of it uttered. While, on the contrary,
many of its members, as was the case with the "Times,"
not only *excused,* but absolutely *encouraged* the wicked

and unprovoked murderers. Such were the circumstances that induced a large gathering of the citizens
(against which so much complaint was made), amounting to about five thousand persons, on the afternoon
of the following Tuesday, in Independence Square.
This meeting was composed of as respectable people
as ever assembled on public occasions, and was conducted with becoming order and decorum. Against
the solicitations of the officers, however, it adjourned
to meet again in Kensington (*which it had an indisputable right to do*), and the greater portion of the
assembly repaired to that district; where, before they
could organize, they were murderously assaulted as on
the previous day, though with still more fatal effects.
At this time about thirty citizens were shot, a number
of whom were killed. Thus, driven to madness and
desperation almost, about twenty of the assailed procured arms, determined to maintain their rights and
revenge their injuries; and against as fearful odds as
men ever fought, they bravely stood their ground until
the victory was theirs. Having succeeded in setting
fire to the houses from which the murderers discharged
their pieces, these last were driven from their imagined
security, and some few fell victims to the vengeance
they had so brutally excited. Read now the published
accounts of these transactions in many of the daily
prints. The writers will be found overflowing with
sympathy; for whom? For the men, who, without
warning or provocation, were instantly shot dead in
our streets? For their mothers, their sisters, their
children? No! Their sympathy is all expended upon

the *murderers* and *their families*. It was an awful
thing that their houses should be burnt ! ! Awful indeed ! ! But it was nothing, that from those houses
were being continually poured out volleys of musketry
and other destructive missiles ! It was dreadful to see
WOMEN and CHILDREN driven from their houses ! ! But
it was nothing that those *women*, and some of their
children, should be engaged in the savage work of aid-
ing their husbands and fathers to murder our innocent
citizens ! It was nothing that some of these women
were discharging stones and fire-arms, with the fury
of savages, upon a defenceless assembly ! ! No. That
was all right ! and because the people put an end to
their barbarity, by getting the mastery of them, they
were abused in the most outrageous manner. Had a
herd of wolves entered that meeting and devoured one
of its members, no one would have spoken against their
extermination. But raw, ignorant, and brutal Irishmen should have been left unmolested to shoot them
down as though they were rabid dogs. Had the venal
press looked on these events with less prejudiced eyes,
it would have discovered more worthy objects than
murderous rioters for its sympathy. It would have
seen a distracted mother meet, at the threshold of her
home, the dead body of her loved son—her almost entire dependence—who, but a moment before, had left
her in health and strength, and full of hope—but now
barbarously butchered ! It would have seen the
mangled bodies of good citizens, killed in the public
streets, by slugs fired from the guns of foreign vaga-
bonds, and the blood of others calling loudly for ven-

geance at the hands of an incensed people. It would have seen the rights of citizenship violated, and the homes of our countrymen made desolate by those who have been driven from their own land by the iron arm of oppression, or the righteous hand of justice. But none of these things could it see, while it could plainly discern women and children perishing in the flames of their burning dwellings!—famishing ones, houseless and homeless, suffering for their faith!—Catholic clergymen, walking the streets in disguise!—blackened bones of the slaughtered, mixed up with smoking timbers!—vultures tearing open the graves of the dead with demoniac fury!!!—and a hundred other things THAT NEVER OCCURRED!!!

CHAPTER XV.

But if the political press, from interested considerations, gave perverted and false statements to the public, much more so did the Catholic religious journals. The following appeared in the "*New York Freeman's Journal*," a paper of the last-named character:

"The natives mustered in overwhelming force, and the Irishmen, now a mere handful, and worn out by the fatigues of the previous two days, *offered no resistance, but were shot without mercy.* Here and there some one with the courage of despair made a stand, *but he too, after a little, was shot down;* and it is sickening to read how *such and such an Irishman*—one named Rice for instance—after keeping a mob of his cowardly assailants at bay for nearly an hour, was finally shot through the back of the head by a "Native," who stole round from the rear.

"☞ ONE THING is now plain—that the promises of the 'authorities' to protect the property of the Catholics is all MOONSHINE! On such promises the Catholics of Philadelphia relied, and their churches and their houses were coolly destroyed without let or hindrance.

The inference is clear. LET EVERY MAN BE PREPARED TO DEFEND HIMSELF AND HIS PROPERTY!!!

From the Bulletin Board of the Irish Volunteer, of Sunday, in letters several inches long.

'*MASSACRE!!*'
'MURDER OF CATHOLICS!!!'"

The "*North American*," then published by C. G. Childs and J. Reese Fry, handled this article as follows :

"The above we take at second-hand from the New York Journal of Commerce. 'The Freeman's Journal,' which uses the language here cited, is a Roman Catholic paper, and no doubt in the full confidence and favour of the dignitaries of that church. It is difficult to comment in temperate terms upon a publication so mean and so atrocious. What would any reader, before uninformed of the true state of the case, infer from this extract and these exclamatory lines? Would he believe that an American and a Protestant assembly had been fired upon, and many of its unarmed members shot dead, or grievously wounded by skulking assassins, whom the Freeman's Journal claims as Roman Catholics and Irishmen? Would he believe that the 'murder of Catholics,' thus announced in glaring capitals, was the instant justice, visited upon the assassins by friends of the victims? Would he believe that, but for the force volunteered by a Protestant community, not one stone would now rest upon another of any Roman Catholic temple in this city? Who would infer any of these facts from the infamously calumnious article from the Freeman's Journal?

"We do not believe that its editor wrote in ignorance of the truth. We do not believe that he wrote unadvisedly as to the spirit of his libellous effusion. He knows, as every man, woman and child in Philadelphia knows, that if the native Americans had not

been shot down by Irish Roman Catholics in the first
instance, there never would have been any disturbance.
He knows that there was nothing to justify the murderous assault upon the meeting of last Monday week.
He may assert that the Irish Roman Catholics were
irritated by the presence and language of their political opponents. What then ? Was not their presence
legal? Was not their language that freedom of speech
which republican liberty requires? If they were rash
in their choice of a place of meeting; if they were
intemperate in their modes of expression; were these
sufficient reasons to excite the other party to shoot
them down like mad dogs ? Such might be reasons if
an Inquisition were in the midst of our city ; but they
are not reasons while freedom of faith and of persons
are guarantied by the spirit of Protestantism and the
constitution of the republic.

"So much for the bloody scenes of last week. As to
the conflagrations, the Freeman's Journal declares
what it knows to be false. From whatever cause the
'authorities' may have failed to protect the two
churches which were burnt, it certainly was not because they belonged to Roman Catholics. Under the
same circumstances, they would have been destroyed,
no matter to what sect they belonged. That they
should have been saved, that with earlier precautions
they might have been saved, no one denies. But that
they were not adequately protected, because they were
Roman Catholic, is utterly untrue, and the assertion
to that effect is a foul and malignant libel. Not the
Austrian troops of the Pope would be, on any occa

sion, more ready than the Protestant citizens of Philadelphia to defend the property of his subjects. They have been ready, thousands of them, since the riots broke out, to peril their lives for that end. They have come forth, freely, boldly, without reward, and have taken up arms in the cause. And now they are told by the arrogant organ of a foreign hierarchy that they are not to be trusted to protect the property of those who live among them?

"The Irish Roman Catholics of this city have a shortsighted counsellor in the Freeman's Journal. There is a worthless rabble in every community, and this community has its share of such a population. That share is a very small minority compared with the entire mass of inhabitants. Yet small as it is, it proved, when its vile passions were aroused, too strong for the Irish Roman Catholics. Without Protestant helpers and defenders, the latter would have been fully overpowered. We assert this as a simple truth. But the assertion is forced from us by the course of the Freeman's Journal. That press has wantonly, shamelessly, ungratefully assailed this Protestant community, and in its behalf we stand upon the defensive. We say only what is necessary to vindicate its character, to prove its love of right, of peace and order, and to stop the foul babbling of those who presume upon its forbearance under unmerited insult."

The "North American," of the 14th May, also gave the following admirable review of the whole subject of the disturbances:

11 *

"Editors of the newspaper press, out of Philadelphia, have been very generally misled by a portion of the press in the city, as regards the true causes of the recent disturbances and the parties responsible for them.   Excessive injustice is done, on the one hand, to the native American party, by charging it as such, with the breaches of law which have occurred, and on the other hand, to the inhabitants of the city proper and the districts *actually adjacent,* by fixing upon them generally the odium of acts committed by comparatively a few persons of the worst class.   With regard to the native American party, this press is not its organ, is not authorized to speak for it, and not being identified with it, can therefore claim to judge impartially.   We shall endeavour, now and in future, so to judge, and in mentioning that party and all others connected, positively or by report, with the recent disturbances, we shall keep facts in view, and leave readers as far as possible to draw their own conclusions from them.

"The first question is, *who began the riots ?*

"The second, *why where they begun ?*

"The third, *why were they continued ?*

"It is a matter of history that meetings for every imaginable purpose have been held of late in this city, without any disposition on the part of any one to disturb the proceedings of them.   Among these meetings were conspicuously those of the Irish Repeal party.   Although thousands of our fellow citizens questioned the moral propriety of meetings, having for their aim an interference between a foreign government and its own subjects, yet not one, who disapproved, ever attempted to disturb their proceedings.   The legal right being acknowledged to assemble peaceably for an interchange of opinion or feeling, or the promotion of any object not adverse to the laws, no one dreamed of opposing the enjoyment of that right, no matter by whom exercised.   But as soon as the native Americans began to hold their meetings, they encountered the opposition of Irish residents, many of them doubtless not even naturalized.   It is not to the point to inquire whether the object of the native American party be just or unjust, liberal or illiberal. It is perfectly constitutional and legal, and that is sufficient. The members had a perfect right to assemble peaceably in any public place.   The expediency of their so doing is another matter.· We agree, so far as the meeting of Tuesday afternoon was concerned, that it was inexpedient.   But on the previous Friday and Monday, there was no good reason shown at the time why they should not meet where they did.   The ground belonged as much to them as to any other persons for the purpose of meeting.   To disturb their meeting in any manner was a gross violation of decency and right.   At that first meeting, then, the riots began ; and by whom were they commenced ?

" We think there is no difficulty in answering this question.   The native American meeting on Friday was disturbed by Irish men and women residing in the neighbourhood.   The interference had no other provocation than the assembling of the meeting in that neighbourhood.   Was this sufficient provocation ? If a

Repeal meeting had been held in any part of the city or county, would the place of meeting—if lawful—have been made the pretext by anti-Repealers for an attack upon it? This is a fair mode of viewing the case. What would have been said, had a Repeal meeting been disturbed for such a cause? We leave those to answer who have endeavoured to extenuate the wrong of the Irish on the day named. With regard to the adjourned meeting at the Washington market (after the meeting in Independence Square), it was rash, unwise, unnecessary, improper. It caused the renewal, as was predicted, of the hostilities of the former day. But then, again, *who* renewed the hostilities? Again we are obliged to answer, the Irish. It was they who recommenced the battle which they had begun. If a certain degree of provocation is chargeable on the other party, still the Irish were the actual aggressors. They had had blood, but they were not satisfied. They were determined to have complete victory. To have and to keep the ground for themselves, to the exclusion of every one who might differ from them politically or religiously, was their resolution, cost what it might. We have thus stated by whom and why the riots began. We have seen no other statement in any quarter, although much has been said to mistify the truth and shift the responsibility.

"With regard to the riots which succeeded the attack upon the meeting of Tuesday, it is just to consider in turn what was the provocation,—not that any provocation could excuse the rioters,—but to remember it is necessary to a full understanding of the case. A.

body of men had been peaceably assembled for a lawful purpose. They were fired upon, first by skulking
assassins, and then more boldly by the same individuals.
Innocent men, the native inheritors of the soil, were
mercilessly shot down for no other offence than the
discussion of a political question. This is the sober,
unvarnished truth. Their friends, exasperated by the
outrage, resented it as far as they could at the
moment. The fever of excitement, always contagious
in a crowd, was caught by that class of worthless persons who are on the skirts of every community, ready
for any mischief. These, finding a pretext for indulg-
ing their wicked propensities, and the occasion to do
so with impunity, took up the affair where the native
Americans had left it. A small body of the latter,
as a party, acted only for the time, and when frenzied
by the ruthless and bloody assaults upon them, on the
defensive. But even that small body took no part in
the subsequent doings of the mob. The persons who
fired the churches were seen by numerous citizens :
some of them were recognised as old convicts by the
police ; many of them were boys ; but none of them
could be pointed out as known members of the American party. It was therefore a motley and depraved
crowd that continued the riots, which the Irish faction
had begun.

" Taking the whole circumstances into view, what
inference must any impartial man draw ? What judgment must he pass ? Shall we forget, as a neighbouring press affects to do, while mourning over the ruins
of brick and mortar ; shall we forget that life was

taken and dreadful wounds inflicted? Shall we forget,
—while we read upon a tottering wall that 'God
seeth'—that if his divine eye rests upon the ashes of
a temple made with hands, and which hands may
rebuild, it looks also upon the lifeless dust of men
whom no power can call into existence? If it be
crime to destroy the sanctuary where the soul seeks
communion with God, what must be the crime which
cuts off a soul from that communion? If sympathy
be demanded for the people who have lost their places
of worship for a few months, what must be the sympathy for those who have lost fathers, husbands,
brothers, sons, friends, for ever?"

CHAPTER XVI.

Retirement of the Military—Disbanding of the Volunteer Police—Hostile feelings still cherished—Funerals—Meetings of Americans—Prominent Speakers—Political misrepresentations and persecutions—Arrests—Onward progress of the Native cause—Celebration contemplated.

IT is now time that we should return again to our narrative. The military from the country, which had poured into the city, in accordance with the governor's orders, after enjoying a very jolly time, at length returned to their homes, to follow their civil occupations, and to recite to their neighbours and children the terrors and toils of their city campaign; our city troops laid down their arms, and resumed the more profitable implements of trade; the Princeton's crew went on ship-board; and the citizen police considered it no longer necessary to continue their midnight duties. In a word, the city and its vicinity were restored to their wonted quiet; and the only remaining indications of a hostile and disorderly spirit were exhibited in the fierce and growling tone of some of the papers conducted by disappointed politicians; the bitter and malignant denunciations of public speakers; and the grim visages of those whose fondly cherished anticipations of elevation to power and fortune were blasted by the waning influence of foreigners in the control of the elections.

(181)

The wicked attempts to destroy the American movement had not only failed, but produced a contrary effect. That movement had received an impetus which was hurrying it onward to speedy and triumphant success. The funerals of those who were so ruthlessly slain were attended by immense concourses of the most respectable inhabitants, and the plainest manifestations of indignation were given toward the causes and instruments of their untimely deaths. Thousands of citizens, who had previously regarded the principles advocated by Americans with indifference, now understood their importance, became the most active and eloquent of their advocates, and united with the republican associations. Ward and mass meetings were held every evening, in every section of the city, and largely attended. At some of these meetings, held in the State-House Yard, and in Chestnut street, in front of Independence Hall, it was computed that from twenty to thirty thousand persons were present. At all these meeting the utmost enthusiasm prevailed. Even in the riotous district, the American cause progressed most rapidly, and immense multitudes assembled, unmolested, to discuss its principles. Mass meetings were also held in almost every county in the state, and in all the principal towns in the states adjoining. All these gatherings were ably, powerfully, and eloquently addressed by persons who had *originated* the American party, and *stood by it in the hour of trial and peril.* Among the most prominent speakers on these occasions, the following names are well remembered:

Jacob Broome,	Lewis C. Levin,
William D. Baker,	John Perry,
William Banning,	William B. Rankin,
Joseph E. Brewster,	Alexander Rankin,
A. D. Chaloner,	Peter Sken Smith,
O. P. Cornman,	H. L. Smith,
H. H. K. Elliott,	E. K. Tarr,
John H. Gihon,	J. B. Strafford,
William Hollingshead,	James C. Van Dyke,
Samuel R. Kramer,	Philip S. White.

Some of these men were most violently abused and persecuted for the active part they took in the establishment and maintenance of the American party. They were denounced in unmeasured terms by *respectable* speakers, who had held high political offices and were seeking others, and who exhibited far more zeal than honesty, in their public speeches; and their names were ridiculed and contemned through the columns of party political organs. And even until this time, they are condemned in certain quarters as rioters, church-burners, and women-killers! The writer of this has suffered more than his full share of this unjust censure, and much of it from parties who have since opened their eyes to the light of truth, and have advocated the principles for which he was condemned. Nay, more; have sought and received office and its emoluments from the despised party whom they denounced as traitors and murderers, and supposed no gallows sufficiently high upon which to have them executed. But we rejoice in their conversion. Paul was sud-

12

denly arrested in a career equally as mad as theirs. He was struck by a "light from heaven." Charity requires the supposition that their light came from the same region. There are still others who were equally as mad as they, and yet would be eagerly welcomed to our ranks. All men are fallible, and the brightest intellect has erred. Let us throw no obstacle in the way of political reformation and moral advancement.

Some few of the Kensington rioters were arrested, but they never received the punishment they deserved, and justice demanded. Several of the American party were arraigned before the courts on criminal charges, trumped up for especial purposes. These men were as innocent of crime as the judges who tried them, and more so than some of the attorneys engaged in their prosecution. There was, however, no intention to do them material harm. It was a good stroke of policy to effect a compromise; and the guilty went unscathed of justice, that the innocent might escape the arbitrary exercise of law.

But despite all opprobrium, opposition, and persecution, the American party not only stood its ground, but continued to receive numerous accessions, until, at the ensuing county election, they astonished the opposition by carrying through their candidate for sheriff. This gentleman, unfortunately, proved recreant to the cause, as did some others who received the native suffrage. The defection of the sheriff, who, with most piteous supplications and even tears, sought the office he received, caused several of the most prominent and efficient labourers to abandon the American party.

During the months of May and June, so rapid and numerous were the accessions to the American associations, that it was deemed expedient to give a public demonstration of their strength and importance on the succeeding 4th of July. Active preparations to that end were immediately commenced and prosecuted; immense sums of money were contributed; and arrangements were completed for the most splendid parade that the city ever witnessed before or since. The ladies entered upon this matter with as much spirit as their male friends, and wrought and procured magnificent banners for all the ward associations in the city and county. A full description of the imposing pageant is reserved for the next chapter.

CHAPTER XVII.

Grand Celebration of the Native Americans on the 4th of July, 1844—Second Declaration of Independence.

THE sun arose on the morning of the 4th of July, 1844, in a bright, clear, and beautiful blue sky; and never did the weather continue more delightful and pleasant, than throughout the day, at that season of the year. It seemed that Providence had resolved to smile benignantly upon the grand celebration with which it was to be distinguished. At an unusually early hour in the morning the city was alive, and at half-past six o'clock associations had been formed and were moving toward the places appointed by the marshal of the contemplated procession. At half-past ten o'clock the procession started, passing over the following streets:

Formed on Arch street, the right resting on Front, countermarched up Arch to Tenth street, down Tenth street to Carpenter, down Carpenter to Fourth, down Fourth to Washington, down Washington to Third, up Third to Master, down Master to Frankford road, down Frankford road to Shackamaxon, up Shackamaxon to Franklin, up Franklin to Hanover, down Hanover to Queen, down Queen to Frankford road, over the stone bridge to Front, down Front to Green, up Green to Sixth, down Sixth to Vine, up Vine to Ridge road,

(136)

out Ridge road to Fisher's lane, along Fisher's lane to Snyder's woods, the place of celebration.

The procession moved in the following order :

Trumpeter of Fame, mounted.

Committee of Arrangement on horseback, ten in number, with broad light blue silk scarfs, badges on hats, and carrying truncheons.

Chief Marshal, Thomas T. Grover, mounted. Aids, Henry H. K. Elliott, and A. Larentree, mounted.

Plough, drawn by two horses, the horses and harness decorated with ripe grain. Farmers leading the horses and following the plough.

One hundred and thirty mounted victuallers of the city and county dressed in white frocks, with light blue silk scarfs and sashes.

Twenty infirm native American citizens, mounted, in citizens' dress.

A barouche containing the President and Vice-President of the New York Delegation, followed by the committee of arrangements from New York, mounted. 65 members.

The banner of this delegation was borne in the barouche. On the top of it were the words "The Bible the basis of Education, and the safeguard of Liberty." Device, the figure of Liberty in a sitting position, with left arm resting on the American shield, horn of plenty at her feet, and the staff and cap of liberty behind her, an eagle flying in the middle ground, bearing aloft the Bible. In the distance a public school-house. On the reverse a full length portrait of Washington, and the inscription, "Seven-

12 *

teenth Ward American Republican Association.   Organized August 13, 1843."

The delegation from Wilmington, Del., numbering
45 members.   The banner and bearers in a barouche.
The banner represented Liberty, with the American
flag, with the inscription " Our fathers gave us the
Bible, we will not yield it to a foreign hand."

The President of the day, E. M. Spencer, Vice-
Presidents and Secretaries, in number seventeen,
mounted.

A barouche containing the orator of the day, Wm.
D. Baker, Esq. ; John Perry, the reader of the Decla-
ration of Independence, and James L. Gihon and Geo.
P. Henszey.

J. H. Gihon and two Assistant Marshals.

The Temple of Liberty, drawn by fourteen gray
horses, led by variously attired grooms, black and
white, the two first representing aborigines.   The
temple was raised on a pediment of four steps—from
which basis arose thirteen columns with Tuscan base.
The staffs of the columns resembling in their propor-
tions the Grecian Ionic unfluted.   The capitals were
of a composite order.   Above the columns was a simple
denticulated entablature with corresponding cornice ;
rising from this was a very elliptical dome surmounted
by a small balustrade, with circular railings.   Upon
each column was hung a scrolled shield bearing the
coats of arms of the thirteen original states of the
union.   Above each column was a golden star representing the several states.   Height 22 feet, 16 feet square
at the base.

The representations of the several states mounted—each man bearing a small banner, with the name of his state, and wearing a blue and white silk scarf.

New York represented by Samuel Ashmead.

New Jersey	"	" Samuel T. Stockton.
Pennsylvania	"	" William Sloanaker.
Connecticut	"	" C. F. Raymond.
Maryland	"	" Elihu D. Tarr.
Massachusetts	"	" Dr. A. Z. Bardin.
N. Hampshire	"	" Joseph Batten.
Virginia	"	" Jacob Mayland.
Delaware	"	" Samuel T. Bodine.
North Carolina	"	" A. Phillips.
South Carolina	"	" Edwin Booth.
Rhode Island	"	" W. G. Snyder.
Georgia	"	" James Hampstead.
Kentucky	"	" David W. Gihon.
Tennessee	"	" C. K. Barker.
Louisiana	"	" J. Jamison.
Indiana	"	" W. W. Fouche.
Mississippi	"	" Henry Warner.
Illinois	"	" Thomas Watson.
Maine	"	" C. K. Frost.
Alabama	"	" John Jordan.
Vermont	"	" —— Parker.
Missouri	"	" Charles C. Ashmead.
Arkansas	"	" A. Thacker.
Ohio	"	" D. Sands.
Michigan	"	" Joseph Chasurt.

Barouche containing the Committee of Relief.

Four barouches containing the orphans of the martyrs, and the wounded in the assault at Kensington. The front barouche bearing a small banner trimmed with crape, with letters painted on it, describing their position.

The Camden, N. J., Native American Republican Association, carrying small bunches of grain—64 in number. Marshal, Mr. Beaumont, and two aids. Brass Band.

Second Ward Spring Garden Association, with banner, bearing the inscription " Liberty of speech and petition," figure of liberty with the American flag—in her right hand a scroll inscribed " Foreign influence is one of the most baneful foes of a Republican Government,"—medallion portrait of Washington surmounted by an eagle, a child on the right of the figure with a staff and cap of liberty; presented by the ladies; 300 members—50 boys. A large American flag, presented by the ladies of the ward, was also carried by this association. A banner carried by the boys, with the motto " The future destinies of our country depend on us." They also carried small flags.

A barouche containing Lewis C. Levin, Mr. Dixey, and Col. Long.

Marshal and aids of the first district, mounted. J. E. Harned, Marshal; assistants Wm. G. Smith and George Snyder.

East Cedar Ward.—Marshall, John Payne; assistants, Robert E. Shultz and John Addis. Banner— The Goddess of Liberty holding in her right hand the American shield, and in her left the American flag. Over her head was an arm holding the sword of justice, surrounded by beautiful flowers; in the back-ground was the ocean and the rising sun; on one side of the circle was the horn of plenty; on the other were the American flags, battle-axes, drums, shells, &c.; the label underneath was "East Cedar Ward;" the one above "American Republican Association." 86 members.

West Cedar Ward.—Banner—A full length statue of Washington on a pedestal, with the Goddess of Liberty descending in a cloud, with the American flag floating over her head. On his left stood Minerva with the American shield in one hand and a spear in the other, the eagle soaring over the head of Washington, and above it the Holy Bible open; the whole encircled with a beautiful gold scroll-work; on each side of the circle were American flags, battle-axes, cannons, drums, shells, &c.; the under label was the motto—"Virtue, Liberty, and Independence;" over the Bible the label was—"Right gives Might." 54 men and 24 boys.

Boys bearing a Liberty cap on a staff, and a small banner worked with a needle, by Miss Province, 10 years of age, representing a dove, with the word "Peace" worked upon it.

New Market Ward Association.—Marshal, J. H. Hurst; assistants, Jno. Barnard and Wm. J. Smith. Band of music. Banner, representing Liberty pointing to a Bible in the clouds, the American eagle in the middle ground. A large silk American flag and twelve small ones, presented by the ladies of the ward. 73 members.

First Ward, Southwark, Association.—J. J. Bishop, marshal; assistants, R. Gaw, J. Feinour, E. J. Young, and Anthony Mitchell. Banner, a figure of Liberty sitting on a rock, supporting a liberty pole, surmounted by the cap, and pointing to a portrait of Washington, with an American flag hanging on one side. The arm of Liberty supporting an open Bible. The mottoes were, "Beware of Foreign Influence," and "We will defend our Country's Rights." 104 members. Large American flag, presented by the ladies. Small banner and flags. A miniature brig.

Second Ward, Southwark, Association.—Marshal, John A. Mercer; assistants, Wm. Shankland, James McElroy, Joseph Day, and Benjamin J. Lyndal; band; banner; the Goddess of Liberty standing beside a pedestal, with an American flag thrown round her as a mantle, and holding in her hands a Bible. Above her, an eagle, grasping with one claw a picture of Washington, surrounded with a laurel wreath, while the other held a liberty pole. From the back of the eagle floated the motto, "Beware of Foreign Influence." Against the pedestal a bundle of rods was leaning, bound round with a fillet, on which appeared the motto, "United who can break us?" A serpent was lying dead at the feet of Liberty, pierced with an arrow, while Fame was soaring aloft, proclaiming the extinction of Papal influence. In the back-ground appeared, on one side, the Temple of Liberty, and on the other a school-house. 120 members—60 boys. A large silk American flag. The association also carried another banner, with portrait of Washington on both sides. Also, a small white banner, with wreath encircling the words "Native American Association, No. 2." Boys carrying a shield, liberty cap, flags, and a banner, with the inscription, "Young hearts, but true."

Third Ward, Southwark, Association.—Marshal, Samuel Sears; Assistants, Norman Davis, Geo. M. Craft. Large silk American flag, surmounted by an eagle, bearing a streamer, with the words, "The Bible is our guide." Banner, representing the Goddess of Liberty enveloped in the stars and stripes, instructing a youth from the open Bible, which stood upon a pedestal alongside of her. Above this, with one claw grasping the edge of the Bible, was an eagle supporting a staff, from which floated a torn flag. From the eagle's beak appeared the motto, "Our flag must be protected." On the panel of the pedestal were inscribed the names of those who fell in Kensington. In the background a school-house. The reverse of the banner had a whole length figure of Washington; motto, "Beware of foreign influence." 108 members. Boys carrying a miniature steamboat and flags.

Fourth Ward, Southwark, Association.—Marshal, Ephraim Palmer; Assistants, E. C. Bonsall, Joseph Hollenback, Wm. Harper, Isaac Dutton, John Miskey. Band. Banner: a rock, on which was an eagle in the act of alighting; on its breast was an American shield —one talon grasped the lightning, while the other held an olive branch and an open scroll, on which appeared the names of the Kensington victims. Above the eagle twenty-six gilt stars were arranged. It was sur-

rounded by a wreath of gilt oak leaves. 166 members.
A large silk American flag.

Model of the merchant ship W. S. Archer, on a
car, with an open Bible at the bow.

Ship Washington, drawn by four bay horses, full
rigged and manned; length 26 feet, beam 6 feet 6
inches, depth 4 feet.

Pilot boat Archer, drawn by two horses. Captain,
G. P. Connell; 15 feet long, 4 feet beam; James J.
Mason, mate.

70 boys. Banner, on which was inscribed, "Juve-
niles of the Fifth Ward, Southwark." Figure of
Washington, &c. Motto, "Our motto is our country's
cause, and that we will maintain." Another small
banner, Bible and eagle upon it, on the American flag.
Miniature sloop.

Two barouches, containing the Delaware Bay pilots.

The Native American Rifle Company of Fifth Ward,
Southwark, in citizens' dress, with military caps and
gold bands. 42 members. Marshal, N. Wills; Assistants, Mr. McBride, S. W. Pierce, Mr. Silbert, and
M. Bruce. Band.

Fifth Ward, Southwark, Association.—Banner:
Liberty supporting an American flag, and pointing to
an open Bible on an altar beside her; two children at
the base of the altar, and Justice on the left; a fillet
and scales on the ground, at her feet, the shade of
Washington seen in the clouds, supported by angels.
190 members, carrying blue wands, decorated with
blue ribbons. Band. A large silk American flag; an
American eagle on a staff, surrounded by small flags.

Water casks. Marshal and Aids mounted. Dr. J. B. Strafford, Marshal; assistants, Joseph Weimer, R. Grimshaw.

First Ward, Moyamensing.—Marshal, Michael Fleetwood; assistants, H. Davis and W. Bishop. Banner: full length portrait of Washington, pointing to a ballot-box on his left, partly concealed by the American flag; inscribed on a scroll were the words, "The remedy is in the ballot-box." Above was an eagle bearing a streamer, inscribed, "Beware of foreign influence." 64 members.

Second Ward, Moyamensing, Association.—Marshal, Aldon James; assistants, Alderman James A. Campbell, William Otley, R. S. R. Andrews, J. T. V. Poole, Jacob B. Goldey. Banner: A full length figure of Washington, standing on the globe, with the star-spangled banner waving over his left shoulder. The staff of the banner, surmounted by an eagle, from whose mouth waved a scroll, with the motto, "No Foreign Dictation." Washington holding an open scroll in his right hand, with the motto, "Beware of Foreign Influence." In the back-ground, a Bible spread open. Band. 70 members.

Third Ward, Moyamensing, Association.—Marshal, John R. Hunn; assistants, D. A. Beard, A. Hentzlewood. A white satin banner, representing a figure of Liberty, holding in one hand the American flag, and in the other, an open Bible. Above the figure, the motto, "Our Country must and shall be free," and below, "Liberty of Conscience." 60 members.

A grotesquely cut box-tree, 150 years old, from the

13

Moyamensing Botanical Garden, borne on an immense car, and drawn by four horses.

Fourth Ward, Moyamensing, Association.—Marshal, Frederick A. Walmer; assistants, John Hawkins and John Lush. The banner represented the Genius of Liberty bearing through the clouds a liberty pole and cap, and the torn American flag, trampled on at Kensington. Above the figure was a bust of Washington, and the Scales of Justice. 70 members.

A large American flag.

Seamen of the Port of Philadelphia.

Men and boys.

Marshal, John Riter; John Williams, assistant.

Banner, representing Washington on horseback; on the reverse, " Free trade and sailors' rights."

Miniature models of the United States sloop of war Peacock, ship Archer, ship Bethel, ship William Penn, sloop of war Dale, ship Colonel Pluck, United States brig Truxton, United States revenue cutter Gallatin.

A number of flags and banners were carried by men and boys, dressed as sailors. 74 men, 30 boys.

Second District Association.—Marshal, E. G. Benson; assistants, H. Horn, and J. Gihon, mounted.

The omnibus Lady Washington, drawn by six white horses, containing old and infirm native citizens of Locust Ward.

Locust Ward Association.—Banner: A full length figure of Washington standing by a table, on which was a ballot-box, inscribed "21 years." A drapery of American flags was beautifully painted above, and falling by the side of Washington. Above was inscribed, "Beware of Foreign Influence." Beneath, "Locust Ward." Marshal, Col. J. K. Murphy; assistants, W. H. Wright, John A. White, Edward Harmstead, John Wilhelm, George W. Watson, and F. G. Bell. Two large silk American flags, and several small ones. 175 members.

North Mulberry Ward Association.—Marshal, Thomas Marsh; assistants, W. S. Peters, F. F. Moreland, Charles Wile, and Peter Wagner. Committee of arrangement in two barouches. Band. Banner, representing young Shiffler, in a kneeling attitude, holding the American flag in one hand, and placing the other to his breast. Under a fold of the flag was a ballot-box. 152 boys bearing various small banners, with appropriate devices.

South Mulberry Ward Association.—Marshal, C. G. Childs; assistants, Andrew Godfrey, William Jordan, Henry Beck. Banner, which represented a shield, was richly wrought, with two historical incidents from Trumbull; Washington in the foreground, under a tree, with several cannons near his feet. The picture above it, on the shield, was the landing of Penn; ships in the distance, with a group of Indians. The whole festooned with the star-spangled banner. Band. 50 members.

Pine Ward Association.—Marshal, George F. Miller; assistants, James H. Stephens, Thomas W. Gilbert. Large American flag. Banner: Liberty standing on a rock on the sea shore, and an angel descending with the open Bible. By her side a shield with a portrait of Washington, surrounded with twenty-six stars,

and she supported a staff surmounted with the liberty
cap. Flags and Carved Eagle. 45 members.

North Ward Association.—Marshal, Joshua L.
Husband; assistants, H. Swift, Mr. Price, M. L.
Wise, Samuel Hill, and J. S. Warner. Banner: A
large rock, on which was inscribed, "Our principles
are founded on a rock—our Institutions on the Bible."
Above this an Eagle supporting the American flag,
the folds of which fell on to one side of the rock; an
open Bible rested upon this, while above a rainbow
spanned the picture, and rays of light were descending
upon the Bible. A portrait of Washington rested
against the rock on one side. Flags. 70 members.

South Ward Association.—Marshal, Dr. Chaloner;
assistants, Robert Brown, E. Roger, T. W. Patton,
Joseph C. Sleight. Banner: The Goddess of Liberty
sitting on a globe; in one hand a scroll, labelled,
"Constitution;" the other supporting an open Bible.
"America—Our Native Land," was inscribed on the
globe. Beside Liberty was an Eagle, with a medallion
of Washington resting on its breast. 60 members.

Lower Delaware Ward Association.—Marshal,
Jesse Burrows; assistants, G. McRedding, J. H.
Pugh, H. H. Simpson, and George W. McDonald.
Banner: A figure of Liberty represented sitting on a
rock, supporting an American flag. At one side a
pillar, against which rested an anchor. Above was
inscribed, "Our Native Land," while below was the
title, "Native American Association." 70 members.

Dock Ward Association.—Marshal, Alderman Peter
Hay; assistants, George W. Prentice, William Alex-

ander, jr., and A. Q. Farr.   Banner representing the tomb of Washington, at Mount Vernon ; hovering over the tomb, the American Eagle, with the star-spangled banner in his beak; in the distance the faint outline of a figure, representing the spirit of Washington. The motto, "Beware of foreign influence."   75 members, 25 boys.

American flag ; miniature ship on a car ; boys with banners.

Walnut and Chestnut Ward Associations.—Marshal, David W. Moore ; assistants, Q. F. Wallace, and J. A. Smith.   Banner : A bust of the mother of Washington resting on a pedestal, with an oak wreath round it.   An eagle hovering over it, holding the American flag in its beak, which fell in graceful folds over the bust and pedestal.   The pedestal had the following inscription, "To Mary the mother of Washington."   In the back ground, a view of Washington Square, with a fac simile of the monument of Washington to be erected in the square.   On the top of the banner the motto, "The only jewels of America should be her sons," and below, "Native American Association." 40 members.

Upper Delaware Ward Association.—Marshal, Joseph T. Whitaker ; assistants, G. W. Jenkins, W. Odenheimer, Joseph Morgan, A. C. Coyle, and J. Raw. American flag.   Banner : A full length figure of Washington standing in front of the Chair of State.   In his left hand a scroll containing the words, "Beware of Foreign Influence."   His right hand resting upon a book labelled, "The Constitution," which was sup-

13*

ported on a Bible upon a table. The American flag neatly festooned at the side and foot of the banner. 80 members.

High Ward Association.—Marshal, E. D. Nutz; Assistants, L. G. Thomas, T. Westcott, and J. Souders. Banner: Washington standing by a table with one hand resting on a Bible. The Genius of America, with liberty pole and cap, appearing on his right hand in a cloud, with an eagle at her feet. The motto, "Beware of the insidious wiles of foreign influence." Black heart wreathed. Inscription, "Our Country always to Heart." Borne by boys. 44 members.

Middle Ward Association.—Marshal, John Wise; Assistants, R. Williams and William Elliot. Banner: Representing a boy standing beside a Bible, and supporting the American flag, over which was, "Our own Native Land," and beneath, "The Constitution of the United States. 60 members.

Third District Association.—Marshal, Jacob S. Haas; Aids, S. Shotwell and David G. Wilson, mounted.

A cenotaph to the memory of those persons who were killed at Kensington, drawn by two black horses.

First Ward Spring Garden Association.—Marshal, John D. Fox; assistants, Benjamin Whitaker, Morris E. Afflick, Henry L. Smith, and John C. Taylor. Banner: Representing a monument, with the American flag over the case, Holy Bible in front, ballot-box under the lower folds of the flag; eagle above, and over all the inscription, "God and Our Native Land."

Small banner carried by boys, with figure of a Bible, and the words, "The light of the world and the guide of the nation." Also, a splendid wreath of natural flowers. 50 members.

Fourth Ward Spring Garden Association.—Marshal, T. J. Herring; assistants, D. P. Vail, J. Dickerson, Jr., J. H. Howard, and Sam'l Simpson. Large American flag, 20 feet long and 10 feet broad, and borne on the shoulders of six men. Band. Banner: The Goddess of Liberty standing in her Temple with the American flag beautifully draped around her, supporting a liberty pole surmounted by the cap. Above the Temple an Eagle resting upon an open Bible, with a ribbon floating from its beak, on which appeared, "God and our Country." The painting was surrounded by a wreath of oak leaves, gilded. Young Natives with banner and flags. 95 members, 38 boys.

Third Ward Spring Garden Association.—Marshal, A. L. Shattuck; assistants, J. H. Amor and John Welsh. Banner: A Temple of Liberty, with the motto, "Liberty of Speech and Right of Petition." On the Temple was an eagle, from the beak of which appeared a ribbon, with the motto, "We have arrived at an important crisis." In the centre was an altar, on which was an open Bible, and above appeared a flying figure of Liberty, with an American flag. American flag. 85 members.

First Ward N. L. Association.—Barouche carrying the banner and flag. Marshal, N. B. Unruch; assistants, Jacob B. Hamilton and Jos. S. Ritchie. An American flag, 144 inches long, by 102 inches wide, the silk of American manufacture. It had for a motto, "Our flag we will defend." The staff was of American cherry, fifteen feet long, surmounted by a gilt eagle, resting on an open Bible, with the inscription, "Search the Scriptures." 40 members.

Second Ward N. L. Association.—Marshal, E. S. Yocum; assistants, Daniel Potts and Lewis Williams, Banner: Washington kneeling at prayer in a wood, with a camp in a distance; over it the words, "May our Land be Immanuel's Land." Miniature model of a man-of-war on a car. 28 members.

Third Ward N. L. Association.—Marshal, Col. Jos. S. Riley; assistants, Benj. Bennet and J. J. Grumpert. Banner: The Goddess of Liberty standing by a pillar, with her staff and liberty cap, and American flag. At her foot, an eagle grasping an olive branch and a shield, with the motto, "Revision of our Naturalization Laws." Above the eagle, a pedestal, with an open Bible, resting upon it. In the background, a statue of Washington, and a school-house. The motto, "Beware of foreign influence." Boys with banner. Boys with flags and banners. 60 members—20 boys.

Fourth Ward N. L. Association.—Marshal, John McIntosh; assistants, John A. Beck, Edwin Sleeper, and Wm. Edmonson. Banner, representing an angel of light dispelling darkness, with the open Bible in her right hand, the American flag in her left. Boys with banners: 40 members.

Fifth Ward N. L. Association.—Marshal, J. G. Flaigel; assistants, Lewis Wolfe, George C. Leidy,

William P. Jenkins, Wm. Stratton, Lewis Burk, I. M. Lye, and R. Taylor.   Banner, the figure of Liberty near a rock on the seashore, with American flag and liberty cap, and the inscription of "God and our Country."   A large American flag.   Boys with banners and flags.   70 members—20 boys.

Sixth Ward N. L. Association.—Band.   Marshal, John Donnalay; assistants, James E. Sulger, H. F. Rasche, and Jesse E. James.   Banner, representing a young man in undress, kneeling beside the altar of liberty, and clasping an American flag, beautifully painted.   An eagle sweeping down towards him, and in the act of placing a laurel wreath on his brow.   At the foot of the altar, the Bible, and in the background, a public school-house.   Over this banner was the motto, "Beware of foreign influence."   American flag.   Young natives with small flags.   130 members —30 boys.

Seventh Ward N. L. Association.—Marshal, Wm. B. Severn; assistants, Samuel Grim, Cephas Custis, Henry R. Russel, John Rookstool, Gordon Wollers, Thomas L. Booth, Geo. Meyers, and John Millington. Banner: The Goddess of Liberty, standing by a pedestal, on which was the American shield, with the open Bible appended to it; her hand resting on the shield, and leaning against the pedestal was an anchor; in her left hand the liberty pole; at her feet the American eagle.   The ground work was very handsome; and on the scroll above, the motto, "Beware of foreign influence."   Band.   Boys with banners and flags.   95 members—26 boys.

Fourth District Association.—District marshal, Joshua Bethel.

Fifth Ward, Kensington, Association.—Marshal, M. Davis; assistants, Calvin H. Test, Henry D. Clayton, Isaac D. Brown, and John Williamson. Band. Banner: An eagle on a rock grasping an olive branch and shield, and supporting by a chain from its beak, a ballot-box, on which was inscribed "Twenty-one years." On each side were stands of American flags. Above the eagle, the motto, "Native Americans," and below, "Our country and our rights, our altars and our God: Instituted March 2d, 1844." Flags. 70 members.

Second Ward, Kensington, Association.—Marshal, John A. Hess; assistants, James Wood, Samuel C. Cox, James McNalty, and George Stetzel. Banner, representing a female in a sitting position, supporting an American shield and a portrait of Washington, and teaching a group of children; an eagle about placing a wreath upon her brow. Inscription, "Beware of foreign influence." Band. 110 members—50 boys.

The torn flag that was trampled on at Kensington, borne on a car, drawn by two horses.

An American flag with the motto, "Though torn still waving."

Boys with banner and miniature ship.

Third Ward, Kensington, Association.—Marshal, Wm. Craig; assistants, Henry Eiciwachter, Clement Callam, Wm. Freeheller, Henry Crout, and David Seely. This banner represented the figure of Justice and Liberty, with the American shield, resting upon

the Bible, between them. Liberty holding the staff
of the star-spangled banner, which waved behind the
group, while Justice held the scales aloft in one hand
and rested the other upon her sword. The shield was
surmounted by an eagle, grasping the Constitution in
one of his claws. Band. American flag. 90 members.

Native Americans mounted. Sloop of war Native
American, 28 feet in length, beam 6 feet 9 inches,
depth of hold 3 feet 4 inches, mainmast 30 feet 6
inches; drawn by 13 horses.

Fourth Ward, Kensington, Association.—Marshal,
John Bonning; assistants, Jos. Smith, John R. Luffberry, John Dysche, Peter Teese, H. Eliakim Hillman. Banner: The principal figure in the foreground was the Goddess of Liberty, supporting with
one hand a bust of Washington, on a pedestal, and
with her other hand holding the American flag. In
front of the pedestal and underneath the bust, was a
shield and a Bible. The back-ground represented a
view of the river Delaware, with the Navy-yard at a
distance, and the river in front of the city. On the
top of the banner was the motto, " We are competent
to make and administer our own laws," and on the
bottom, " Beware of foreign influence."   75 members.

The fishermen of Kensington, with the fishing boat
Independence, rigged and manned, on a car drawn by
four horses.

Fifth Ward, Kensington, Association.—Marshal,
John R. Myers; assistants, Adam Hempshire, Adam
Henricks, Samuel Husted, Samuel T. Hay, and

Thomas Merrit.   American flag.   Band.   Banner
representing the Goddess of Liberty pointing to an
open Bible, on an altar beside her.   At the feet of the
figure, an eagle holding a scroll, on which was inscribed,
" Washington's Farewell Address."   65 members.

North Penn Township Association.—Marshal, Mr.
Rheinich ; assistants, Geo. Miller, and Edward
Maupay.   Banners.   20 members.

Germantown Association.—Marshal, Isaac E.
Leech ; assistants, John W. Harmer, and Wm. Stad-
dleman.   Banner representing the death of Lawrence.
American flag.   40 members.

District of Penn Association, No. 1.—Marshal,
Peter K. Young ; assistants, Wm. Harney, and
Robert Able.   Banner representing an eagle on a
pedestal, holding a Bible ; American flag on the
pedestal, with medallion portrait of Washington.   30
members.

Manayunk and Roxborough Association.—Marshal,
Charles T. Jones ; assistants, Alonzo Robb, Francis
Kirkpatrick, and Nelson Paxson.   Banner : repre-
senting Liberty clad in the American flag, holding a
medallion portrait of Washington.   45 members.
Thirty mounted farmers.

The streets during the whole line of the procession
were densely crowded, while along the entire route the
windows and balconies of the houses were occupied by
ladies, showering bouquets and wreaths, and waving
their handkerchiefs in token of admiration.   Taking
it altogether, a more brilliant display could not well

be imagined.   The line took upwards of an hour and a quarter to pass, and the head of it did not reach the place of celebration until four o'clock in the afternoon.   Between six and seven o'clock, P. M., Mr. E. M. Spenser, president of the day, called the meeting to order, when Mr. John Perry read with much effect, the Declaration of Independence.   He was succeeded by Mr. Wm. D. Baker, who delivered a brief, chaste, and beautifully written oration.   After which, Mr. Wm. D. Barnes read " *The Declaration of American Republicans of Philadelphia City and County, July 4th, 1844.*"   It was as follows:

" When, with a sudden and unpremeditated movement, large masses of citizens cast at once aside the political opinions, that, maintained with the warmth of honest conviction, have before divided and alienated them, and quietly and resolutely combine for some national object, if the principle of our government be true, it is inconceivable, that the reason of their movement should be silly, or that in the impulse which urges, they have not felt the real anguish of a hidden sting.   The political moralist often thinks he sees the error he prates about, the people always know they feel the wrong they thus act against.   Wide spread must be the knowledge, and unendurable the nature of the evil, that, at the moment the trumpets of all parties are sounding, unites the people in a multitudinous American combination.   Originating in love of country, we have the good of our country as our end.   And that all men may know this, we make our

14

public declaration of the wrongs our country suffers, and the remedies we seek to apply.

" We hold that the civil liberty we enjoy is sure and uncontrollable, because by the popular possession of the elective franchise, that civil liberty is popular power. Upon this principle we declare, that it behoves us to be cautious and considerate how we admit new persons to a share of this power, common prudence forbidding it, until their minds, tempers, and inclinations are habitually and fixedly subjected to the fundamental maxims on which our liberties depend.

"We hold that as the elective franchise continues the power in the hands of the people, it is the life of our liberties, which are thus made to depend upon the popular will. And, therefore, while we are ready and willing to extend to the oppressed of all lands, who choose to seek refuge under the mild and liberal humanity of our government, the enjoyment of those inestimable benefits it returns us, we will take care to preserve that popular will, an American national will, not debase it into the alloy of an intermixed will, half foreign, half national, thus lessening and deteriorating in its nature our national birth-right; Esau-like parting with our portion, without Esau's excuse.

"We hold to prostitute this franchise, is certainly to take from the people their power and to destroy the institutions of our country. And, therefore, it is to be guarded as a blessing most holy, from whose sacred precinct we, its inheritors, are enjoined to put afar off, not only all danger, but all probability of danger.

"We, therefore, declare, that to open the elective

franchise with unlimited confidence to all foreign in-
comers, after a five years' residence, is repugnant to
the duty and dignity of our position as American
citizens.

"It is admitting to a share of national power, to a
voice in our National Council, and to a direction in
our national policy, a man who is a stranger by birth,
not only to our land, but to all our customs, to all the
habitudes of our national mind, to all our national
prejudices, to all our national views, to all our national loves, to all our national unity of purposes,
which are the slow growth of many lives, and can
neither be rudely deracinated, or violently implanted
by a brief five-year labour.

"That among the foreigners who have been elevated
by the ennobling gift of the elective franchise, is constantly displayed the convincing proof of this proposition. Their hearts and their lips overflow with
insolent impieties towards our constitution. They
blaspheme the names and things we hold in most reve-
rent honour, and sell their votes for office.

"There is daily poured upon our shores and spread
throughout our coasts, a population, festering and em-
poisoned with all that train of disorderly appetites,
which the errors and miseries of their state in the old
world have inevitably engendered. They are at five
years made partakers of the very life of our national
being, by law; and systematically, within five days,
without law.

"Against this early and easy naturalization, both
legal and illegal, we do most seriously protest; we

protest even in the case of those whose misfortunes and whose virtues claim our tender sympathies.

" We protest alike against all; Because five years is too short a time to nationalize the heart, instruct the understanding, and fix in a national habit the mind of any man; Because, a foreign demagogue can, at this moment, command the votes of tens of thousands of these naturalized voters, in favour of whom he pleases to select for any office in the people's gift; Because, foreign dissensions, foreign factions, foreign influences, and foreign corruptions have, by means of these laws, been introduced into the heart of our liberties ; Because, foreign parties are springing up among us to our shame, our confusion, and ultimately our downfall; Because, it is selling our highest and dearest honour too cheaply for population; Because, it is a lessening of the dignity of the American character; Because, it is allowing other people to grow upon us, not we ourselves upon other people ; Because, when it pleased heaven to make us free, it was that we were fit to be free, and therefore fit to govern ourselves, a decree it has not yet pleased Him to pronounce upon any other nation of the earth, and, therefore, we hold it wise, expedient and fit, that we govern ourselves without the interference or assistance of these others.

" We, therefore, children of the land, fully impressed with the necessity of such action, do declare that we advocate a residence of twenty-one years in the land, as the indispensable condition to be fulfilled by every foreigner before our honourable birth-right be in any way bestowed upon him. To this principle, forgetting all party distinction, and recollecting only our country, we most solemnly pledge and devote ourselves, neither will we faint or falter until our end be accomplished. Lest while we enjoy the blessing of Reuben,—' Oh! Reuben, my first-born, my might, and the beginning of my strength, the excellency of dignity and the excellency of power;'—we also fall under his curse,— ' Unstable as water, thou shalt not excel.' "

Mr. William Hollinshead next read Washington's Farewell Address.   The utmost harmony prevailed throughout the day and during the proceedings, and although more persons participated than had ever taken part in any public celebration in the city, no accident occurred.

At the time the meeting adjourned, accessions had been made to the assembly, of ladies and others from the city, in omnibuses, carriages, on horseback, and on foot, until there was not less than twenty thousand persons on the ground.   The celebration closed with the most brilliant display of fire-works ever witnessed in the country, under the superintendence of Mr. Samuel Jackson.

14*

CHAPTER XVIII.

Certain parties not pleased with the Fourth of July Celebration—Apparent determination to produce new outbreaks—Arming of the Church of St. Philip de Neri—Excitement occasioned thereby—The sheriff calls out the military—Arms removed from the church—Arrest of Charles Naylor—Attack upon the church—Liberation of Naylor—The Hibernia Greens compelled to leave the building—Murderous fire of the military.

BUT the peaceable and tremendous demonstration of American feeling exhibited in the magnificent celebration of the Fourth of July, though highly gratifying to all good citizens, produced contrary effects in the minds of other classes of the people. There were certain prominent politicians who saw in it a death-blow to the success of their lofty aspirations, and others, of more humble pretensions, feared they were about to lose for ever that "balance of power," which alone gave them consequence, and which they considered of too much importance to surrender without the most desperate struggles. The giant adversary, that had so suddenly risen in their midst, must be destroyed at every hazard. Whilst this existed, they were powerless. Nothing was more inauspicious to their hopes than the peaceful calm that had followed the Kensington storm, which they had raised. Another tempest must be aroused; but where and by what means, was a perplexing question. Malicious abuse,

(162)

unfounded prosecutions, and repeated persecutions had failed to provoke the native Americans to lawless aggressions. They kept on steadily in the even tenor of their way, daily gaining both moral and numerical strength. Catholic churches were undisturbed, and noisy Irish politicians were permitted, without molestation, to boast, bluster, and threaten to their hearts' content. The American party was fully satisfied with the triumphs it had achieved, and the clear prospects of future conquests.

Notwithstanding all this, the Catholics were determined, if possible, to create new disturbances, and thus arrest the onward progress of the cause they dreaded. Hence, vague rumours were put in circulation, that their churches were threatened, and publicity was given to ridiculous anonymous communications, doubtless written by themselves, to that effect. No one believed these silly stories. The whole public knew that there was no disposition anywhere to disturb Catholic or any other churches. Yet, upon the pretence that they were in danger, the Catholics applied for and received permission to arm their religious temples. In doing this they accomplished the desired object—that of instigating new outrages.

On the afternoon of Friday, July 5th, the people in the neighbourhood of the church of St. Philip de Neri, in Queen street, between Second and Third streets, Southwark, saw arms and ammunition carried into the church. The circumstance was regarded as strange, unnecessary, and inexplicable, and consequently produced considerable excitement. As the story spread, crowds collected about the church, and serious indications were given of an approaching disturbance.   About 8 o'clock in the evening matters had assumed so threatening an aspect, that a committee of citizens called upon the sheriff, urging his interference to preserve the peace of the neighbourhood. That officer repaired at once to the scene of excitement, after having called upon Major-General Patterson for the aid of the military.   Upon his arriving at the church, the crowd demanded that the arms should be removed ; when the sheriff, with Aldermen Hortz and Palmer, and a few citizens, entered the building, and after a search of some half an hour, returned to the street with twelve muskets, several of them heavily loaded.   These were declared to be all the arms that were in the house.   This did not satisfy the people, who had seen more carried in, and another search was consequently made, which resulted in the discovery of seventy-five additional muskets, some of them so heavily charged with buck-shot, ball and slugs, that they could not have been fired without danger of bursting ;   and also a number of axes, hammers, bludgeons, knives, pistols, a keg of powder, and box of cartridges.   The sheriff and the committee, however, very prudently, to prevent an immediate outbreak, which otherwise would have occurred, kept this fact concealed from the now immense crowd that had collected in the street, and it was not generally known until the following morning.

At about eleven o'clock, Captain Hill's company of City Guards arrived on the ground, cleared the street, and posted sentries at the corners, when the people quietly dispersed. Early on the following morning, however, they began to assemble again in vast numbers, and at two o'clock, P. M., Queen street, from Second to Third, was densely packed. Soon afterwards, General Cadwalader rode in on horseback, and addressed the multitude, urging them not only to refrain from violence, but to disperse. In reply to questions relative to the authority by which the arms were taken into the church, he stated that an order for twenty muskets had been issued by authority of the governor, and that they had been delivered before he had any knowledge of the order. His attempts to persuade the crowd to leave the place were unavailing, and he withdrew without having accomplished any good. In relation to the subject, a few days afterwards, the "Ledger" very judiciously remarked:

"Mr. Dunn, who is a brother of the priest of that name, got an order from the governor for twenty stand of arms. Whether the governor was apprised of the object to which these guns were to be applied, we know not. The probability is that he was not. More fire-arms, procured otherwise, swelling the number to some eighty, were taken into the church. Now we are of opinion that there is about as much use for guns in a church, as for a powder magazine under it. And if the Reverend Mr. Dunn had reflected properly, that his mission is one of love and not blood, he would never have been a party to the matter. But the guns, all or part of them, were there by authority, either special or implied. If by special authority, there they ought to have stayed until the proper civil officers had come to the discreet conclusion that a church is not an armory or a fort; a conclusion which a very little reflection would have brought them to. Or if the guns were there by no special authority, their removal was a very simple matter. But in either case, there was no cause for public excitement—no cause for a mob."

But the public mind had not yet got completely over the agitation produced by the Kensington butcheries. The volcano that had been smothered, needed the aid of no great means to cause it to burst forth with renewed fury. The mere carrying arms into a Catholic church would have excited no especial attention, but for the wanton attack of the Catholics in Kensington upon unoffending citizens. It was that attack that created the apprehension in Southwark that some dread mischief was in contemplation. They were actually alarmed (perhaps unnecessarily), and hence the deplorable consequences that followed.

As the day advanced, the crowd increased in numbers and in turbulence. It had begun to assume the character of a lawless mob, and threats of violence were freely indulged. At 7 o'clock the sheriff arrived with a posse about one hundred and fifty strong; drove the throng from the front of the church; and stationed lines of men along Queen street, from Second to Third, thus preventing all ingress to the square. During the evening the military was reinforced by the Mechanic Rifle, Washington Blues, Cadwalader Grays, Markle Rifle, City Guards, and Junior Artillerists, the latter bringing three field-pieces, which they so stationed as to command all the avenues to the church. About eleven o'clock, Gen. Cadwalader, with a platoon of men, charged upon the throng in Second street, below Queen, driving them down to Christian street. Similar measures were pursued up Second street and along Third street. In Third street, the mob became more noisy than ever, and commenced throwing stones at the military. General Cadwalader then gave orders to fire, and one of the field-pieces was levelled at the crowd; when Mr. Charles Naylor, who was one of the sheriff's posse, sprang into the street and countermanded the order. He was immediately arrested by command of the general, and confined in the church. His act, though contrary to military discipline, prevented the discharge of the gun, and the destruction of many innocent lives. Toward morning, quiet was gradually restored, and the military mostly retired, leaving the Mechanic Rifle and Hibernia Greens to guard the church. The stationing of the latter named Irish company for this purpose was as injudicious, as the command to fire musketry down a densely crowded street was rash and hasty. Both these acts, together with the arrest and confinement of Naylor, only tended to fan the fire that was only smouldering, into a furious and terrible conflagration.

Early on Sunday morning the crowd, which now had among it some of the most reckless and turbulent spirits in the city suburbs, again began to gather in front of the church, and at eleven o'clock threats were made to attack it if Mr. Naylor was not released. An old four-pounder, lashed upon timber wheels, was brought up and pointed at the door, and would have been discharged had not some person thrown water upon the priming. A large log was then obtained, which was used as a battering-ram. With this the panels of one of the front doors were forced, and an entrance into the church effected. Mr. Naylor was then released, and getting upon the steps, he made a short address, urging the people to keep the peace and retire to their homes. He was loudly cheered, and marched by a great multitude to his residence in Fifth street above Walnut, where he again conjured them to act like worthy and peaceable citizens.

The crowd next demanded that the Hibernia Greens should be sent out of the church, and it was agreed that they should leave with the pans of their guns opened and unprimed. They came out, however, with their muskets not only primed, but many of them cocked also. They were followed up Second street by some of the most riotous of the mob, who groaned, hooted, and even pelted them with stones. At the corner of German street, one of them, named Gallaher, turned and fired into the crowd, wounding a boy. The company then broke and fled in all directions. Gallaher was pursued to Sixth street, where he took refuge in a house at the corner of Small street. After several pistol shots were fired into the house, he was seized, dragged into the street, and terribly beaten about the face and head. Some citizens then carried him to the Southwark Commissioners' Hall, where he lay a long while in the rear basement, apparently dead. He subsequently recovered.

An exaggerated report having obtained circulation that the Hibernia Greens had fired upon the people, the excitement was increased thereby, and crowds hurried to the church in greater numbers than ever. The police having command of the front door to keep away the mob, a battering-ram was applied to an eighteen inch wall between the church and a dwelling-house on the west. This soon gave way, and the crowd rushing through, forced the side door and windows and filled the building. In the mean time, another cannon, mounted on wheels, and loaded with pieces of iron, spikes, &c., had been posted in the yard in the rear, and discharged against the wall. A number of the prominent members of the American party, who had volunteered their aid to protect the church and preserve the peace, were in the interior when the mob entered, and, mounting the altar, appealed to the rioters in an eloquent manner to desist from further violence. Speeches to this effect were made in the church, in the streets, and adjacent lots, by Messrs. Thomas D. Grover, John Perry, Lewis C. Levin, C. J. Jack, and others. These gentlemen succeeded, not only in allaying the excitement, but in organizing a committee of one hundred gentlemen in the church, mostly prominent native Americans, in whose hands the crowd agreed to intrust the building, and who, on their side, had pledged themselves that no further mischief would be done. The mob was then gradually retiring, having accomplished no material injury to the

15

building nor its fixtures. The greatest damage was done by rude boys on the outside, who had amused themselves by throwing stones through the windows.

As certain interested parties ascribed these disturbances to the American party, and their published statements to that effect have still left the impression on many minds, in distant places, the following honest testimony of the "Public Ledger," of July 8, is given to correct the error. The editor remarked:

"The present riot was commenced by a desperate set of men, who were opposed by the Native American party. The latter were posted to guard the Church of St. Philip against the attacks of these men, belonging to no party, actuated by no principle, not even that of blind revenge; but moved merely by a reckless disregard of all civil restraints, and rioting for the love of riot."

News soon reached the head-quarters of the authorities that the church had been violently entered, when a preconcerted signal (eight taps on the State-House bell) was given, and the military under command of General Cadwalader, amounting to about two hundred men, instantly assembled in Independence Square. In a little time their line was formed, and the brigade, with music playing, were on a rapid march for Southwark. Thousands of persons were drawn together by the alarm on the bell, and followed the military, attracted by their warlike display and the music of the bands, perhaps all of them as orderly and peace-loving citizens as any in the community. The head of the line entered Queen street at Fourth, about 7 o'clock.

The street was blocked up completely with a dense mass of human beings, not one of a thousand of whom had the slightest disposition to riot. Upon this mass, which was materially increased by the throng that accompanied the soldiers, the military pressed with hot and needless haste; some of the officers evidencing greater excitement than the most furious rioter on the ground. As the crowd was forced down Queen street, it became more closely packed, in consequence of those in the rear not instantly giving way, and it would have been quite as impossible to dam up the river with straws, as for the people to retreat as fast as was expected. Still the soldiers pushed forward, the crowd endeavouring to give way as rapidly as possible. The officers brandished their swords, and indulged in the most violent, profane, and threatening language, while the men pricked the crowd with their bayonets, not even sparing the police, who had volunteered to protect the church and assist in preserving the peace. Thomas D. Grover at this time received a bayonet thrust from one of the soldiers. When near the corner of Second street, Captain Hill, of the City Guards, who was urging forward his men, and venting threats of slaughter, was necessarily resisted by the crowd, who could not possibly escape, when he gave the word to fire, which was obeyed; the most of his men, however, wisely and mercifully, discharging their muskets in the air. Notwithstanding this, and the people were flying in all directions, a second volley was poured into the crowd; both volleys making sad havoc among the multitude. Among those who witnessed this transaction, were many who boldly attributed the excitement of Captain Hill to the influence of liquor; but he subsequently, upon his examination before the civil tribunals, ascribed it to the effect of a blow received upon the back of his head by a stone thrown from the crowd. Be this as it may, there was not in that vast multitude one dispassionate person, who really believed there was an actual necessity for the murderous fire that then destroyed the lives of innocent and peaceable citizens. The military had been severely censured for their inefficiency and tardiness of action in the riots of May, and they seemed determined to make amends for doing too little in Kensington, by doing too much in Southwark. In the former place there was actual need of military interference; in the latter their useless presence was acknowledged on all hands to be the cause of the dreadful disasters that occurred. Had their aid not been invoked, there would have been no actual disturbance, and no cause to mourn the untimely deaths of respected and valuable people. These are truths that it was then pronounced treason to declare; but justice requires them now to be chronicled as matters of history, which hundreds of witnesses still live to attest.

Quite a number of persons were killed and wounded by the fire of the military, and the excitement became intense. This was by no means allayed by the exposure of several dead bodies in the Commissioners' Hall. Threats were now loudly made against the military, and it was quite evident that the most serious difficulties were yet to come. Most of the people, who

had been drawn to the place from idle curiosity, retired
to their homes, or to discuss the matter at a safe distance; whilst another class, less peaceably disposed,
repaired to the Wharton market, at the southern border
of the town, to plot retaliation and mischief against
the military. These were reckless, resolute, though
turbulent men, who displayed a degree of courage,
which, employed in a good cause, would have done
them great credit. They obtained muskets and an old
cannon, which they loaded with pieces of iron and
glass, chains, spikes, nails, and every villanous thing
that they could obtain and use for the purpose, and
having determined upon their plan of operations, proceeded up Front street to Queen, the wheels of their
gun-carriage being muffled. The night was unusually
dark, and favourable to their purpose. They posted
their gun in Queen street, after drawing a rope across
the street in front of it, to prevent being surprised by
the cavalry, and at about half-past eight o'clock poured
a deadly fire into the military; this was instantly returned by the artillery at Second and Queen streets,
and thus a fight commenced that continued until between two and three o'clock on the following morning,
when the cannon of the rioters was captured. After
retreating from Queen street, the latter had quietly
repaired to the corner of Third and Christian streets,
and, taking the same precautions as in Queen street,
they discharged their piece up Third street. They
were here charged upon by the cavalry, who were
thrown into confusion by rushing against the rope.
At this moment the match was again applied to the
15 *

cannon, but fortunately it burnt priming, and was secured. During all this time small arms were discharged by the military, and by the rioters from the tops of houses, alleys, and corners of the streets. One of the rioters, named John Cook, was killed in Queen street, while engaged in firing the cannon. John Guiger, a member of the Germantown Blues, was instantly killed at the corner of Third and Queen streets, and H. Troutman, of the same company, was mortally wounded, and died early next morning. These were all the killed of the military, though twenty-three others were wounded, some of them seriously. There were four persons instantly killed and many severely wounded, by the first fire of the military. During the entire disturbance, the killed and wounded numbered more than fifty persons, some of whom were shot in their houses whilst taking no part in the affair.

CHAPTER XIX.

Another threatened attack upon the military—Action of the Southwark aldermen and commissioners—Withdrawal of the troops from the Southwark district—Arrival of the Governor, and unnecessary military display—Arrests of rioters and others—Legal examination—Testimony of John Dutton.

EARLY on the morning of July 8th, the crowd again assembled in greater numbers than ever at the Wharton market, until it swelled to upwards of two thousand men, well provided with arms and ammunition, and having in possession a large gun mounted on wheels, which they obtained on the wharf. They were organized with proper leaders, and boldly declared they would drive the military from the district. They even deputized persons to visit the sheriff, and other authorities, to announce that the military would be attacked at four o'clock in the afternoon, if they were not withdrawn. This was their fixed determination, and would have been executed, and a terrible slaughter effected, if their demands had been refused. Having understood that reinforcements of troops were expected by the New York steamboat, at two o'clock, they dispatched a party to the river to prevent the boat from landing. She, however, came without the troops, and was unmolested. A guard was also stationed to pre-

(175)

vent shot being taken by the military from the Southwark tower.

In the mean time the commissioners of Southwark
held a meeting, and passed the following resolution :

" *Resolved*, That it is the opinion of this Board of
Commissioners, that the continuing of the military
force now in this district, has a tendency to keep in
existence the present excitement, and that if the troops
now occupying the public streets of Southwark are
not withdrawn, there will probably be an additional
shedding of blood."

The aldermen of the district also assembled, and
addressed the following communication to Major-
General Robert Patterson :

" SIR: From the representations of a number of
citizens of this district, we are persuaded that if the
military are removed from the neighbourhood of St.
Philip's Roman Catholic Church, in Queen street,
order will be immediately restored, and the citizens
will protect the church. We will give our every exer-
tion for the furtherance of the object. We do not
hesitate to say that peace and good order will be immediately restored."

The sheriff likewise addressed the military commander as follows :

" SIR: The aldermen of the district of Southwark
have given me notice that they are abundantly able to
protect the property and peace of the district of Southwark. I learn also, that the commissioners of that
district have officially made a similar declaration; and
in view of these facts, I would respectfully suggest

that the troops now having charge of St. Philip's Church, Southwark, should be relieved. You are therefore requested to order them to such other point as you may deem best suited to their comfort and repose, holding them in readiness to act, when necessary, at such places as may be menaced."

Accordingly, an order was issued, and the military at three o'clock withdrew to the arsenal on Thirteenth street, in the city proper. The fact being announced to the crowd at the Wharton market, they shortly dispersed, after loud cheering. The church was left in charge of the aldermen and commissioners, who placed about it a strong civil posse. Quiet was now restored, and the only persons in the neighbourhood were curious little squads examining and commenting upon the marks on the trees and houses along Queen and Third streets, made by the bullets and other missiles of the rioters and military. The governor arrived in the city by the afternoon train, after having issued orders to the military, who came pouring into the city daily for nearly two weeks, from every section of the state, until upwards of five thousand soldiers were here under arms. The head-quarters of the commander-in-chief were at the Girard Bank, in Third street. The city was under martial law, and many citizens were challenged by sentries, and even placed under guards in passing between their dwellings and places of business. This ridiculous farce was kept up long after any person imagined there was the shadow of necessity for the display, if indeed there ever had been. But the governor finally wearied of the cam-

paign, and the city was relieved of what had become
an almost intolerable nuisance. The military from
abroad were relieved, and permitted to return to their
homes, having uselessly neglected their business,
wasted much precious time, and put the state needlessly
to an enormous expense. They were highly compli-
mented, however, for their gallantry, which in a measure compensated for the loss of health, comfort, time
and money. In the mean time many arrests were
made on the charges of riot and inciting to riot.
Among the latter class arrested, were Col. J. G. Wat-
mough, Wm. P. Hanna, and the editors of the "Sun"
and "Native American" newspapers, Messrs. Lewis
C. Levin and Samuel R. Kramer. Most of these
charges were founded upon the most flimsy pretexts,
and after the parties had been subjected to vexatious
annoyances, they were discharged.

The subject of the Southwark riots may be dismissed
with a few extracts from the testimony upon a legal
examination, before a Court of Oyer and Terminer,
Judge Jones presiding:

John Dutton, being sworn, said: "I was in Southwark on the evening of the first commencement of the
riots (Friday). When I first went upon the ground
there was a crowd immediately in front of the church;
the sheriff and his posse were endeavouring to keep the
crowd back, who were gathered in the street in a considerable number. I heard that arms had been taken
into the church in the course of the afternoon; the
people were anxious that these arms should be brought
out. I saw the sheriff; he stated, in front of the

church, that twelve muskets had been brought out, and called upon some of those present to take charge of the guns. I took one of the guns, and I asked the sheriff as he passed me, whether there were any more arms or men in the church: he stated there were no more arms, and but Priest Dunn and the sexton in the church. We took the guns to the watchhouse, and when I returned, the mob were crying for the rest of the arms to be brought out. I thought the excitement was produced by the fear of the guns being there, and not knowing for what purpose they had been placed there. In passing through the crowd, I heard the committee spoken of, and that the sheriff had consented to the search taking place. The committee did not appear to be chosen, but the first twenty that entered formed the committee. After entering, the sheriff took our names, and informed us that he made us his posse. He also told us we would have to remain all night, but they did not seem willing to do so without searching it. The sheriff said it was illegal to search the church, but if we would remain until morning he would prosecute the search with us. The priest here interposed, and hoped we would act like Christians and gentlemen, and have confidence in what had been told us by the sheriff and himself. He said there was no danger, as neither arms nor men were in the church. At this time a door in the vestibule was opened by some one, and two Irishmen were seen with loaded muskets and fixed bayonets. We passed into the room, and we found muskets stacked along the floor. There was a guard placed over these men and muskets, and the rest proceeded into the main body of the church. We found other Irishmen in the front of the lower story, and at the foot of the stairs. There were ten in all in the building bearing arms. The priest had said positively there were no arms nor men in the church. Mr. David Ford, one of the committee, asked Priest Dunn, if there were more arms, ammunition or men in the church. To the first two questions I heard him distinctly answer, "No!" I asked some of those found in the church why they had not given the church up to the civil authorities. The priest answered, that with fifty men he could defend it against a thousand. We were anxious to search some closets, at which the priest demurred. We did search, and in these a keg of powder was found and some pistols. On finding these articles we were incited to search another closet under the stairs. The priest stated that it only contained private property belonging to his brother and some few things belonging to himself. On this account he declined opening it, on various excuses. On our positively insisting upon it, the key was found, and we discovered some fowling pieces, containing loads eight fingers deep. Cartridges were also found, some with eight, nine, and ten buckshot or slugs. Wm. H. Dunn addressed us, and said that for fear that erroneous impressions should go before the public in regard to the sheriff, his brother or himself, he would state that both he and his brother had told the sheriff the number of arms in the church; that he had received these arms at the order of Gov. Porter; that he held a commission from General Hubbell, constituting him a captain of men to defend that church, and that on the evening of the 4th of July, he had one hundred and fifty men in the church, drilling them. The sheriff said that Priest Dunn had told him and the aldermen, that were with him, the number of arms in the church. He expressed a doubt of the expediency of the measure, though there was, perhaps, nothing illegal."

This testimony of Mr. Dutton, which was confirmed by other witnesses, gives anything but a favourable aspect to the conduct of the priest and prominent members of the Catholic church. It shows clearly, that while the American citizens were peaceably engaged in celebrating with appropriate ceremonies the anniversary of American Independence, certain Irish Catholics had turned their meeting-house, dedicated in the name of the Messiah to the worship of God, into a citadel and military drill-room, and were engaged in preparations for a civil war. What was the necessity for this warlike preparation? No person had ever threatened to disturb the church of St. Philip de Neri. It has never been pretended that any such threat was made. Why then were Irishmen secretly armed and drilled within the sacred walls of the church? Surely the Irish Catholics gave ample grounds for apprehension to the peaceable citizens living in the vicinity, by this strange, inexplicable, and inexcusable conduct. Let, then, the lamentable results of that conduct be justly ascribed to the misguided men by whom the Southwark disturbances were provoked.

16

Mr. Dutton furthermore testified:

" On Sunday morning about 10 o'clock, saw a cannon drawn up in front of the church, but knew none that were around it. I got upon the cannon and asked what was the matter. I was answered that Mr. Naylor was in the church, and they wanted him to be released. I urged them to desist from firing the cannon, saying that I believed from what I had seen that it was the wish of those belonging to the church to have it destroyed or burned. I told them that if Mr. Naylor was not liberated in half an hour, I would deliver myself into their hands. I was answered by a brickbat alongside of my head. I left the spot and went to the hall, and in about a quarter of an hour I heard that Mr. Naylor was liberated. * * * [Sunday afternoon.] I came out of the church for some purpose, and saw the military approaching. Spoke to Colonel Bradford, aid to General Cadwalader, to the effect that I did not think there was any necessity for their presence ; that all was quiet; and that the mob they had attracted would be the cause of any disturbance that might occur. The military proceeded to clear the street very precipitately, and this, with the crowd brought down by them, I thought apt to create an excitement. I considered the haughty, overbearing manner of the military tended greatly to excite this feeling. I was myself standing at the iron gate of the church, having been pushed into that position by the military, and was determined to maintain my post as the sheriff's officer, till he should give me a discharge. While in this position we were pressed very

closely by the bayonets of the military. I conceived
the position we occupied to be dangerous, and I begged
for my life, stating at the same time that I was a
sheriff's officer. The officer in command of the line
said he did not care for that; that he knew no one in a
citizens dress. The sheriff came up at that moment,
and one of the committee asked to be discharged. We
were then hemmed in by the bayonets of the soldiers.
When the sheriff spoke the military fell back. Mr.
Grover then passed out, gave up the possession of the
church, and at the head of the committee passed down
Queen street. Before reaching the corner they were
also charged upon by the military. I saw General
Cadwalader order the company to take possession of
the church, and afterwards saw him when the firing
commenced, which took place before more than twenty
of the committee, consisting of about a hundred, had
passed the lines. I was standing in front of the church.
A person was brought up from the corner of Second
street as a prisoner. General Cadwalader was then
in front of the church. They wanted to take this man
into the church; some one objected. General Cadwalader was appealed to, who said he could not station
guards over prisoners—they must be shot. Alderman
McKinley said he had better mount the red flag at
once. The sheriff was on the ground at the time of
the firing. He said he hated this firing. I proceeded
out of the lines without any difficulty."

CHAPTER XX.

In making quotations from the evidence given in court respecting the disturbances at the church in Queen street, our object is simply to confirm by legal proof, some of the statements made in the body of this work, that have been and yet are subjects of dispute in certain quarters. That the St. Philip de Neri church was armed without sufficient reason, and that the arming of the church was the sole cause of the calamities noticed, are facts admitted on every hand. The expediency of invoking military aid under the circumstances, the conduct of the military, and the consequences resulting from their action, are matters less clearly and generally understood. Numerous witnesses have testified that no actual disturbance had taken place, or was even threatened before the military made their appearance; that their presence alone caused the outrages that followed; that when they temporarily withdrew, peace and quiet were restored; that their return was productive of violence and murder; and that their final withdrawal was attended with the most happy results. All the evidence in the case clearly proves that the civil authorities were at all

(184)

times abundantly capable of preserving the church from violence, and the district of Southwark from riotous disorder. As the arrest of Mr. Naylor had much to do with the outrages that subsequently transpired, it will be well to notice his own testimony in relation to that event. As this is extremely lengthy, we can do no more than make a few extracts bearing directly on the points at issue. After naming the circumstances that brought him into the scene of disturbance, he having been enrolled by the sheriff as one of his posse, Mr. Naylor thus describes the manner of his arrest on the night of Saturday, July 6th:

"At the time of my arrival on the ground, Queen, from Second to Third street, was clear, and lines of police with a small number of the soldiers, were formed across Queen at Second and Third streets, to prevent the people from passing into that section of Queen street in which the church was situated; and this continued to be its condition during all the time I was present. I met the sheriff just at nightfall in front of the church; and from that time until about 10 o'clock at night, a period of full two hours, I never left his side. There was nothing to do; there was no danger that I saw. There was no resistance, no opposition, nor even a shadow of opposition to the arrests of the sheriff, nor to any of his movements. There was a number of people gathered outside of the lines of the police and military, attracted apparently by curiosity to gaze at the spectacle. Occasionally there was a cheer—a hurrah among them. Now, some one would cry out, 'hurrah for the natives!' Then, at times an

16 *

expression would be used which would give offence to
the police, and an arrest would be made. But beyond
what I have mentioned, there was no breach of the
peace or disturbance, nor any act done or threatened
indicating a design hostile to the peace or property
of the community. I saw no acts by which evil dispositions were manifested. About half-past nine o'clock
a messenger came to the sheriff with the information
that some general (I think General Cadwalader) would
be on the ground in about an hour, stating that 'his
troops were ready to march at their armory, and that
the general had gone to equip himself.' Upon this
message I remarked to the sheriff, 'this is a good
joke; here is a droll confirmation of all you have said
about the tardiness of the movements of the military.
Rioters, with incendiary dispositions, could burn down
all the churches in town, whilst a general is putting
on his finery.'

"Some time after ten o'clock, I accidentally became
separated from the sheriff. The crowds around the
corners had begun to disperse and go home, and all
was quiet and peaceful. Whilst I was looking for the
sheriff, a few minutes after I lost him, I saw the general that I have just named, coming down Queen street,
on horseback, alone. This was his first appearance.
He passed through the lines of the police and soldiery,
and dashed in among the people in Second street above
Queen. He was greatly excited, rode on the footways
and almost into the very doors of the houses; swore
at the citizens standing at the doors of their own
homes; bestowed on the people the most opprobrious

epithets; declaring that he had brought two cannons on the ground; and swore repeatedly, with strong emphasis, that he would shoot them down if they did not instantly disperse. Almost every sentence contained an oath. He behaved with the utmost recklessness; and nothing seemed to be left undone or unsaid, which could have a tendency to excite resistance to him. But there was none offered that I saw. Wherever he went, confusion, alarm, and dismay followed; and the people fled, on all sides, as fast as they could. The peaceful and orderly character of the people was clearly manifest by their forbearance. But I saw at once that such conduct would inevitably end in difficulty, if not in bloodshed. The police, many of them, became alarmed, and were heard to say, 'The general is drunk.' I had never before seen such conduct in a man reputed sane.

"I saw that something was to be done. I sought the sheriff diligently, with the determination to advise him to remove General Cadwalader from the ground. With this resolution I followed the general up Queen street to Third, inquiring as I went for the sheriff. As soon as the general arrived at Third street, without a word of warning that I heard, he rode in among the people assembled in that street, north of Queen, with the same recklessness that had characterized his course in Second street. He rode over the police, and the same exclamation as in Second street, was heard from them with regard to his condition. He called on the police to make arrests. I was with them all the time

assisting. Several arrests were made, and the citizens
fled before us and the general, as fast as they could,
without resistance. Men were arrested wholly without
offence. In a minute the assemblage of citizens in
Third street, north of Queen, was dispersed, and not
a man remained, that I could see, within fifty yards
of our line and the military.

"I had just returned from the chase of the citizens,
and was seeking the sheriff, when I heard his voice in
Third street. General Cadwalader was then near him
on horseback. He was in a state of great excitement, and swore 'By God, he would fire.' The sheriff
replied to the general, 'Don't fire; there is no necessity for it; I will go up to them and disperse them.'
A voice of a small boy, some thirty or forty yards
further north, was then heard to say, 'fire and be
d——d; what is the use of swearing so much about
it?' This seemed to exasperate the general still more,
and he wheeled with the quickness of lightning, and
swore whilst wheeling, 'By Jesus Christ, I will now
fire.'

"Perceiving, as I thought, a frantic purpose in the
general to fire, I had given up the pursuit of the
sheriff, and was retracing my way back again to the
line of police. At this moment I heard the order to
fire. Knowing that this fire was wholly unnecessary,
directed against peaceable citizens, and that the *sheriff
himself was exposed to it, and would in all probability
be shot*, I advanced a few paces, in front of the guns,
and imploringly exclaimed, 'No, don't fire! don't

fire!' They did not fire. After a pause of a moment,
the general asked who had dared to countermand his
orders? Unwilling to shrink from responsibility, I
left the street, stepped up on the curbstone, by the side
of the head of his horse, and replied in a quiet, cour-
teous, and subdued tone, 'I, general; I begged you
not to fire.' The general exclaimed, 'Arrest this
man.' Several voices were now heard to say, 'He is
one of our police.' The general replied with great
warmth, 'By G—d, he must be arrested.' Then
some one said, 'It is Mr. Naylor, one of our police,
and the sheriff's friend.' This seemed to exasperate
the general still more, and he swore again, 'He must
be arrested, and made an example of.' In a calm,
quiet tone, I said to my fellow police, 'Gentlemen,
obey orders; I am willing to be arrested; I will go
with you anywhere.'"

This testimony of Mr. Naylor was corroborated by
many witnesses. Indeed so general was the feeling in
his favour at the time, that had not his release been
effected on Sunday morning, results more serious
than any that occurred would have been the consequence. General Cadwalader had an unquestioned
right to order the military to fire upon the citizens;
nay, to wantonly slaughter the curious crowds that
stood gaping about in the vicinity of his command;
and Mr. Naylor was guilty of a breach of discipline
in interfering against the exercise of the sanguinary
disposition that he supposed was being manifested.
But that interference saved the lives of innocent

people, and prevented calamities, the extent of which it would be difficult to determine. It was not, therefore, surprising that a party of men, even though they were rude and turbulent, appreciating the humane and generous motives of Mr. Naylor, should demand and even unlawfully liberate him from the prison in which he was needlessly confined. This accomplished, they were satisfied, and manifested no further disposition for riot or disorder. That General Cadwalader was influenced by improper feelings, we have no disposition to aver, though we think his conduct at the time was hasty and injudicious. He has since proved himself a useful soldier, and upon the battle-fields of Mexico has done " the state some service." It is due to him too, that we should give his version of the circumstances above related. He says:

" The sheriff directed me to disperse the crowd wherever seen ; which I intended to do. In riding forward in front of the line, seeing that the mob were not disposed to disperse, but to resist, I endeavoured by my manner and language, unusually decided, to apprise them of my intention to use force, if necessary. They cried out, ' fire and be d——d,' and threw a shower of stones. Having been convinced that all who were not participating had withdrawn from their position, I directed Col. Pleasanton to order a platoon of musketry to be fired, deeming it unnecessary to fire the whole force, and fearing that the discharge of the piece of artillery would reach persons beyond the range of those immediately connected with the assault."

The testimony of the general in regard to the arrest of Naylor, is substantially the same as that given, except that the exclamation of Naylor, " Don't fire," was " in a loud voice, and was made in an excited manner, calculated to have an injurious effect upon his command 'and the civil police." His order to arrest Naylor, and determination to have it obeyed, was given to test " whether there was mutiny or intention to side with him among the sheriff's posse," in which case, he says, "it was my intention to have wheeled a platoon and fired upon them."

The testimony of Thomas D. Grover gives a correct account of the assault upon the church on Sunday; the character and disposition of the rioters; and the arrival and conduct of the military. In company with Mr. Levin, Mr. Grover proceeded about noon to the rear of the church, where they found a crowd of men and boys, mostly boys, with two guns, one of which had been fired against the wall of the church. Mr. Grover says:

" I got on one gun and he (Levin) on the other, and eventually succeeded in getting them quiet. They were in the act of priming when we mounted the cannon. I proposed to take the gun away, and this seemed rather a stumper to them. They said they would, if I would let them fire once. But I said, ' No, that would never do.' So we took the gun to the wharf, where I drove a nail into the touch-hole. When I came up I saw a crowd rushing up Second street to the hall. I went in, when the people formed a meet-

ing, and called me to the chair. A resolution was
passed to appoint a committee of twenty-five from each
ward to support the law and defend the church. I
went home, got two flags, and came to the church, the
flags waving. There were thousands in Queen street.
I went into the church. Then those outside got a battering-ram at the door. We fought them off for some
time; got no assistance from those outside, except
three or four, and had I twenty men such as Johnson
and another, I could have prevented the mob from
getting in. I told them they could not get in that
way except over my dead body. They went away and
battered down a wall, when they came in in crowds
through the side doors and windows. I don't think
there were over twenty men who worked with the battering-ram, and some of them appeared intoxicated.
I went all over the house, wherever I apprehended
violence. I saw a young rascal with a couple of
bunches of matches holding against the wood-work,
and then I got mad and threw half a dozen boys out
of the windows. The mob broke the crosses, &c., and
we had to humour them, and finally we succeeded,
after their curiosity had been gratified, in getting them
out.   After we had got all quiet, it was quite an hour
before the military came, and they brought a large collection of people with them. Word came to me that
General Cadwalader wanted to see me. I went out.
The general asked whether I could get the men out.
I said I could. He said, 'Will you get them out?' I
replied, 'I have said so.' At this time the Grays

charged with their bayonets. My back was towards them, when the point of a bayonet struck me under the shoulder, and cut through my coat. After I left the general, and was going into the church, I saw a soldier with his gun cocked, and his piece half levelled three times, as if he was going to shoot a reed-bird. I saw men in the ranks who I did not know belonged there. When I got the men inside formed, we came out two and two. I said to the general, 'We deliver the church up into your hands, and are now clear of responsibility.' I requested him to see us safe out of the lines, and he said it should be done. The people were very much agitated. I tried to pacify a stout man who was there, when I saw an officer run out toward the mob, six or seven paces in advance. I let go of this man, and immediately he clinched the officer's sword, and they stood wrestling. Then some three or four men stepped out and made a charge with their bayonets on this man. Then came a couple of stones, one of which struck one of the men on the cap, and as soon as this was done, the word fire was given by some one in my rear. They fired. I turned towards the soldiers and saw a man with two or three muskets pointed at him. I believe he was in the church with me. When the smoke cleared up, I saw two or three men down. I went over to the north-east corner, and scarcely had I got there when they fired in that direction. When I first went down to the lines, after leaving the church, the crowd were doing nothing—perhaps using violent language. When the

17

officer went out into the crowd with his drawn sword, I
think I could have cleared that street in fifteen minutes.''

The officer here alluded to was Captain Joseph Hill
of the City Guards, whose own testimony differs very
little from that of Mr. Grover, in regard to the circumstances which induced him to order his men to
fire.   Immediately after this fire, a crowd rushed to
the Commissioners' Hall, and seized the muskets that
had been taken from the church.   Others collected at
various points.   Cannon were obtained upon the wharf.
And at between eight and nine o'clock the fight between the military and the mob commenced, the particulars of which have already been given at sufficient
length to answer the objects of this work, and give to
the reader a correct impression of the facts.

CHAPTER XXI.

Prosperity of the American Party—Order of the United Sons of America
—Newspapers established—Spread of American principles—Recent
elections—Americans becoming more alive to their own interests and
the importance of a distinct Nationality—The charge of secrecy
answered—Americanism proscriptive—Plan of nominating candidates
by the old parties—Clannishness of Catholics and Foreigners—Objects
of Americanism.

POLITICAL partisans and aspirants availed themselves
of the Southwark disturbances, to bring reproach upon
the American cause. Denunciatory speeches were
delivered and articles written against the prominent
members of the native party. To these were ascribed
the disturbances, which it was notoriously known they
were the most active and persevering of the citizens
in endeavouring to suppress. All these efforts of the
opposition, however, failed in accomplishing the
intended object. The American cause had received a
fresh impetus, and was now beyond question fixed upon
a firm and enduring basis. To stay its onward course
was utterly impossible. Among its most ardent supporters were the best members of the community.
The necessity for their action, and the maintenance
of their principles, was no longer a matter of question.
Day after day the ranks of the old parties were thinned
by dissenters to the new organizations. The order of
the " United Sons of America" was established in
every neighbourhood, and their weekly meetings were

attended by hosts of respectable citizens. Immense multitudes assembled in town meetings to express their approbation and admiration of the American measures. Two new daily newspapers, the "American Advocate," edited by Messrs. W. D. Baker and H. H. K. Elliott, and the "Native Eagle," by Gen. P. S. Smith, had entered the field to discuss boldly and ably the principles and purposes of the new party. This was no longer treated with contempt by the old partisan leaders; but many of them changed their plans of operation, and sought and implored its influence. Its high destiny was seen and felt and acknowledged on every hand. The foreign politicians fought hard against its onward progress; but their attempts were like the dying struggles of drowning men. They caught at every floating straw, but one after another they sank beneath the rolling waves of popular opinion. For a number of years the American party held the balance of power, which had formerly been so greatly abused by naturalized voters, and succeeded in correcting very many of the abuses of which it had complained, and the removal of which had been the main object of its organization. Some of the most determined of its original opponents enrolled themselves beneath its triumphant standard. And finally, it has become the most formidable political association of the day. It is no longer a mere local organization. It is not confined in its operations to the large cities in which it originated, nor to any one section of the American republic. Wherever true American feelings exist; wherever the actual lovers of America are

found; wherever the honest friends of American institutions and purely republican doctrines live, in the
whole extent of our vast country, there exist the ardent
admirers and zealous advocates of the established
measures and principles of the American party. These
are freely, openly, and eloquently defended and
advocated by the leading public journals of the
country; by members of all the state legislatures,
representatives in Congress, and the most learned, able,
and powerful senators in the United States Senate.
In Philadelphia county the Americans control the
elections, and almost all the offices, great and small,
are held, as they should be, by those who were born
on American soil. Naturalization papers cannot now
be obtained by immigrants fresh from ship-board.
" Cradles of Liberty," to rock infant foreign paupers
in a few hours into full grown American freemen, can no
more be found in the rendezvous of political tricksters.
And the alien vote no longer possesses sufficient value
to be considered worth the purchase. Nor will the
onward progress of the American cause be stayed,
until not only all for which its original advocates contended, but even more, shall be accomplished. As
well might we attempt to arrest the rapid course of the
lightning's flash. All the offices in the gift of the
people, throughout the length and breadth of the land,
will be held by native citizens, and the naturalization
laws will at least be amended as proposed, if not
entirely abolished. At the late state election in Pennsylvania, the American candidate for canal commissioner received a majority of more than one hundred

17 *

and forty thousand votes over his opponent, who was a foreigner, while the American candidate for governor also received an overwhelming vote. The same has been measurably the result of the recent elections in almost every state in the union.

But these are not the sole triumphs of Americanism. Had it only succeeded in establishing itself as a political institution, and elevating its members to political station and power, its work would have been incomplete. It has already accomplished more than this, and is destined to accomplish still more. It is *Americanizing the people of America!* It is giving to them national characteristics of which they have heretofore been unmindful. No people in the world have been more regardless of their own true interests. None were ever known to appreciate so little their own productions, their own talents, genius, and industry. They have entertained a morbid hankering for everything from abroad, and they could discover merit in nothing that was not foreign. Our manufactures, equal to any in the world, must have a European stamp to obtain an American market! Our fashionable American ladies could not wear a bonnet unless made by a "milliner from Paris!" Our limping dandies must have their delicate feet encased in French calfskin, shaped by a French shoemaker! And our superb artists could not obtain a living until they had made the tour of Europe! At our theatres, Europeans of doubtful reputation and mediocre abilities, have been received with open arms, applauded without measure, and rapidly enriched, while our own superior talents and acquirements, with decency and virtue combined, have been left to starve in obscurity! Even a common juggler, born in Philadelphia, to obtain patronage there, was compelled to announce himself as the "Fakir of Ava;" and young girls from our city suburbs, who ride horses around the ring of a circus, must be represented as Spanish *Señoritas*, or French *Mademoiselles*. They were compelled to be anything but what they were, Americans, in order to succeed. In this latter respect the lower ten thousand who patronize the circus, are but imitators of the upper tendom, whose admiration of an opera depends altogether upon its being foreign, and especially *Italian!* Now this sickening affectation for things foreign, has not only sent millions of dollars from the country to enrich strollers from abroad, but it has absolutely justly subjected the American people to the ridicule of all Europe. Political Americanism is curing this evil. It is encouraging American talents, arts, science, and industry, and it will succeed in convincing the entire people, that there is no imaginable thing needed for subsistence, comfort, and luxury, that cannot be originated in our own country as well, if not better, than in any other. We shall soon need few importations of any kind, and the sooner the better. Already our wealthy gentlemen can ride in carriages and on saddles of our own manufacture. Their dames begin to think their floors can be as prettily covered with carpets made at Lowell as by those brought from Brussels or Turkey. Some of them, too, are giving their daughters good American educations before they furnish them with French, Spanish, and Italian teachers. And their young bloods of sons can drink Jersey City cider without its being labelled Heidsick. Even American actors and actresses have lately been applauded, who had never been on a *London stage*, or taken lessons in the *French school!* Let the American party go on with the good work, and all Americans will become proud of America! It will soon become as unpopular to praise foreign as it has been domestic products.

It is unnecessary to devote much space in answering the silly objection that Americanism has become a *secret* political institution, and is therefore dangerous to the liberties of the country. Some of those who most strenuously advance this objection, have had too much experience in secret associations to believe that it possesses the weight of a feather. It is a species of special pleading in which the advocate himself has no confidence. It is, indeed, the forlorn hope of a beaten adversary. Whether the American associations are really secret associations or not, is a question concerning which the writer pretends to know nothing. Admitting, however, that they are, the objection against them on that score is fallacious, and comes with a very ill grace from the parties by whom it is made. Who are the objectors? Old political wire-workers, log-rollers, and pipe-layers, both Whig and Democratic. These are the men who denounce the secrecy of Americanism! To those who have ever been behind the scenes of the political stage, this denunciation can only excite ridicule and contempt. How has the machinery of the old parties been worked for many years past? Openly and publicly? No. The people before the curtain knew as little about what was going on behind it, as the inhabitants of another world! Who have been in the habit of nominating the candidates to fill the offices in the country? The people? Far from it. The *people* were never consulted; nor had they any hand in the matter. The *modus operandi* was very simple, and can easily be explained. The whole work was not only done in *secret*, but very few were permitted to take a part. Some half-dozen individuals in a certain district, rendered important to their party by their aptness at political chicanery, trickery, and rascality, would assemble at an appointed time in the upper story of a groggery, quietly, slyly, mysteriously, and *secretly*. None could be admitted to their counsels who were not in their confidence, and bound, soul and body, to their interests. A bottle of brandy and a bunch of segars having been procured, the nomination of candidates for the approaching election became the subject of conversation and controversy. Each one of the little secret caucus had "an axe of his own to grind," and each was willing to play into the other's hands, if he was certain of having the favour returned. Each one had friends to choose, who either were or could be pledged to his interests, or used for especial purposes; and after a very pleasant evening's meeting, during which the bottle had been

several times replenished, a tolerably complete ticket
was determined upon. This was the *primary* meeting. Thus was the *original nomination* made. The
next movement was to get this nomination sanctioned
and approved by the clubs of the different wards.
These assembled as did the first caucus, without much
public notice; and sometimes their meetings comprised
no more than three, four, or half a dozen of the most
worthless residents of the wards. These men were
not difficult to manage by the master spirits, who kept
them in leading-strings. Hence, at the ward meetings, the original members of the primary meeting in
the groggery, with such others as they might select,
very readily became *delegates* to the general nominating convention. Of course, the ticket originally
determined upon, was then placed before the party for
its sanction and approval at the general election, and
he who refused to sustain it was at once decapitated.
He was accounted a traitor, and as such denounced.
The only choice left for *the people*, was, whether they
would vote for a whig or a democrat; for between the
candidates themselves there was little or none, and
generally, they were the very last persons in the community whom the general public would have ever
thought of selecting for the responsible stations to
which they aspired! In some districts, instead of the
delegate system being adopted, farces called *primary
elections*, were held. In these cases the original wire-
workers had only to secure for judges and inspectors
men who were known to possess consciences sufficiently

elastic to allow them, without severe suffering, to render such returns as were desired. If this could not be accomplished, it was quite an easy matter to surround the primary polling places with rowdies and shoulder-hitters, Irishmen with blue sticks and hard fists, or such other characters as would keep all respectable citizens away. Hence, in every instance, the result was the same—the nomination of the ticket chosen by the original secret caucus. And yet the principal actors in these innocent little political schemes and operations are now making a terrible hue and cry against the secrecy of American associations, and their great danger to the welfare of the country! How dreadfully honest have they become, and how monstrously sudden has been their conversion! One who knew them well, would have supposed they had long since " sinned away the day of grace." The times of miracles have not yet past. It is not denied that in the American meetings all the members (and they number thousands instead of couples and half-dozens) have the liberty to nominate candidates, and vote for whomsoever may have been nominated. When did the Whigs or Democrats ever enjoy such privileges, or make their nominations with such publicity?

The allegation that Catholics are excluded from American political associations has already been hinted at. It may be true, or it may be false. If true, it furnishes no just cause for complaint. Any association of men, for whatever purpose organized, is justifiable in excluding those whom it prefers not to fellowship. But in excluding them, it gives no just ground for the charge of religious proscription. If it does, how will the Catholics justify themselves against this charge? They never pretended to desire any fellowship or communion with Protestants. There is no affinity between them as religionists, and so far as politics are concerned, the Catholics were unquestionably and undeniably the first religious sect that ever combined to interfere with the national, state, or municipal elections of our country. This is a fact too well corroborated to afford a subject for controversy. If, then, Protestants have adopted their policy, circumvented them by so doing, and deprived them of the "balance of power," of which they boasted and injudiciously employed, let them blame themselves and none others for the opposition they provoked, and the certainly desirable results that have followed.

There can be no more ground for objecting to Protestants excluding Catholics from their associations than for Irishmen excluding English or French, or for Americans excluding all who are not "native and to the manner born." Even in our country we have long had Scotch Thistle Clubs, Irish St. Patrick's societies, English St. George's, and Welsh St. David's associations, and purely French and German organizations, and no complaint has been made from any source. If such institutions are proper, and the fact has not been questioned, then is it right and proper that the Americans should have associations exclusively their own. Right or wrong, they have such associations, and their name is legion. There is no secrecy in regard to that fact, nor yet to their objects. They aim to destroy all undue foreign influence in our country. They maintain that Americans should hold all offices of honour, trust, and profit in America; that the natives of the country are the best qualified to govern it; in a word, they have resolved, and they have adopted the best means to accomplish that purpose, to AMERICANIZE AMERICA!

CHAPTER XXII.

THE foregoing chapters were in press when a circular, written by Hon. John Cadwalader, and intended
to influence especially the Virginia gubernatorial
election, was placed in the author's hands. This circular is characterized by gross misrepresentations,
unfounded statements, and abusive declarations. Charity induces the supposition that it was conceived and
brought forth in ignorance; but even this furnishes no
sufficient apology for falsehood and slander. Nor is
the respectability, high standing, or wealth of a writer
an adequate excuse for unjustifiable denunciations of
men who, at least, imagine themselves actuated by
pure motives and labouring in a praiseworthy cause;
nor yet for attributing to them sentiments which they
abhor, and conduct of which they are innocent.

Mr. Cadwalader's circular is published in reply to
certain inquiries concerning the American party, pro-
pounded by Mr. Henry E. Orr, in a letter, dated

(206)

Washington, 6th March, 1855. In this letter Mr. Orr flatteringly observes : " There is a peculiar fitness in interrogating you, and peculiar reason why the people of Virginia and the South should rely with abiding confidence upon the truth of any opinions you may advance." Never did Mr. Orr fall into a more palpable error. The " peculiar fitness" in inquiring of Mr. Cadwalader concerning the true character, principles, and purposes of the American party, is the " *peculiar fitness*" that one would exhibit in making inquiries respecting the merits or worth of an individual from his most bitter and malignant enemy. And there would be just as much " peculiar reason" to anticipate a truthful answer in the one case as in the other. The circular of Mr. Cadwalader gives a sorry earnest of the " peculiar fitness" of that gentleman to answer the interrogations of his friend. The following is Mr. Orr's letter :

" Washington, March 6th, 1855.

" DEAR SIR :—As a Virginian and democrat, I feel much interest in the gubernatorial election which is soon to take place in the Old Dominion. This feeling of interest has been much increased by the changed aspect of public sentiment, regarding certain classes of our fellow citizens, and the privileges by them enjoyed under present laws ; and because, whatever may be the motives of members of the American party (so called), it seems leagued too closely with, and receives too unanimous support from the abolition higher-law men of the north, to be confided in by the south, or by the south's true friends, the national democratic party of the north.

I desire, therefore, to have your views upon the following questions, viz. :

1. Whether the know-nothings and abolitionists have not

acted together in sending a nearly unanimous abolition delegation to the next Congress, from the anti-slaveholding states, and whether they have not fully and freely combined in every state election, for state and even county purposes, except in the state of New York?

2. Why the know-nothings and Sewardites did not coalesce in New York?

3. The reason why the know-nothings are unfriendly to William H. Seward?

4. The probable effect of know-nothingism on southern interests; and

5. Its tendency and effect in a general or national point of view?

There is peculiar fitness in interrogating you, and peculiar reason why the people of Virginia and the south should rely, with abiding confidence, upon the truth of any opinions you may advance. You but recently emerged from the heat and smoke of a battle against this new element of danger to the peace and dignity of the republic, if triumphant in its ultraism. Besides, you stand at a geographical point from which to judge of these things accurately, and I trust you may find it convenient and proper to speak in the hour of our common country's peril, and before the south participates in the inauguration of error and intolerance.

Your friend, sincerely,   HENRY E. ORR.
Hon. JOHN CADWALADER, Philadelphia, Pa."

Some of our readers will remember an anecdote that a few years past went the rounds of the newspapers. Two Irishmen entered a restaurant, and sat down at a table to enjoy the luxury of a beef-steak. "Jemmy," says Patrick, "this stake has a most excellent *flavel.*" "Flavel—flavel," says Jemmy, "and what's a flavel?" "Sure," replies Pat, "and is it possible, Jemmy, that you don't know what a flavel is?" "By my troth and I don't." "Well, then, Jemmy, a flavel is a flavel." "Is that a fact?" says Jemmy; "as sure as long as I lived I never knew what a flavel was before." The questions of Mr. Orr, and the replies of Mr. Cadwalader, are well illustrated by those of Patrick and Jemmy. "Please tell me, Mr. Cadwalader, what a know-nothing is." "Why," says Mr. Cadwalader, surprised at the ignorance of his friend, "a know-nothing is a know-nothing." "Indeed," rejoins the delighted Mr. Orr, "I never knew before what a know-nothing was." But Mr. Cadwalader was less sensible than Pat in the anecdote. He must unwisely proceed to discuss at great length the subject concerning which he proves himself most emphatically a "know-nothing." This is said, as has already been remarked, from a charitable disposition to put the best colouring upon the monstrous perversions, to use no harsher terms, that distinguish the circular under consideration.

There is a singular oceanic creature called the "Squid," or, as some designate it, "Cuttle Fish." When it wishes to conceal itself, it emits a black fluid in quantities sufficiently great to darken the waters many acres around. Mr. Cadwalader's circular reminds us very forcibly of the squid. He has endeavoured to conceal himself, or rather his ignorance, by the emission of an immensity of verbiage. This, however, may be accounted for in the fact that he is a lawyer, and has acquired the common habit of drowning a few ideas in an ocean of words, in order that his wondering clients may be satisfied that they are getting the full value of their money. It is this peculiarity of the circular, perhaps, that has induced the democrats to

18 *

give it so wide a circulation. Supposing there must
be much wisdom and knowledge, or at least something
concealed in the multitude of words that it comprises,
they have sent it forth into the world without giving it
a very careful perusal. Had they penetrated its dark
waters, they would have found a creature even less
significant than a squid. And had Mr. Orr desired
correct information respecting the American party,
he might have found thousands in the country whose
" peculiar fitness" to answer his inquiries far exceeded
that of Mr. Cadwalader, and who had less " peculiar
reason" to disguise the truth.

The letter of Mr. Cadwalader commences and closes
with *abuse* of the American party, a means only employed by those who are conscious that their positions
cannot be sustained by arguments and facts. We give
our readers the full benefit of his language :

" The know-nothings originally assumed their denomination
as a disguise to conceal their identity with the former self-
denominated native American party. This identity, which they
were never able to conceal under the thin veil of attempted
secrecy, has lately been acknowledged in their open organization, under the name of Americans. When the native American party was originally organized, every one of its members,
who had previously professed membership of the democratic
party, was rigorously exscinded from the democratic organization. The native Americans, after the late presidential election, were aware that the remembrance of this would prevent
them from obtaining an avowed reinforcement from professing
democrats, who, though ready covertly to desert their party
organization, were not yet prepared to renounce openly the
party's name, and at once abandon all hope of restoration to its
ranks. The name of native American was, moreover, odious

from the recollection of the scenes of lawless outrage by which it had been disgraced when the Catholic churches were burned in 1844. They, therefore, devised the scheme of a secret organization."

"Native Americanism soon, however, burned its own wings, in sacrilegious fires lighted with its own hands. Religious persecution, promoted by arts of unprincipled demagogues, resulted in acts of such violence, as had, in Europe in a less enlightened age, disgraced the day of St. Bartholomew. We, who were born and bred Protestants, and have never had any religious affinity with those who follow the Catholic faith, or been connected in any association with its professors, recur with pain, mortification, and shame, to the recollection of the ruins of smoking dwellings and churches which were burned in 1844 by incendiaries, who would have prostituted and debased the proud name of American if their impudent invocation of it had been authorized—as thank God it was not, and never has been! The disgrace of the so-called native American party, consequent upon those outrages, induced the federalists to postpone their intended fusion with them, and retain for a few years longer the name of whig. But though the whigs thus retained their name until 1852, they never, in the mean time, scorned alliance with the native American party, even after it had become known by the opprobrious, but well deserved name of 'church-burners.' Whenever a local election could be carried by a temporary fusion of the native American and whig parties, they were always found united against the democracy."

The most vindictive political writer could not have concocted paragraphs with less regard to truth. To denounce a large body of citizens, as respectable, intelligent, honourable, and high-minded as that which originally composed and now constitutes the American party, exhibits a sad want of good taste and generous sentiment. That bad men have advocated the American principles, there can be no doubt; but who will

pretend to deny that among the leading democrats of
the country, may even now be found those who are a
disgrace to the American character ? But this would
be an insufficient reason for members of American
associations to assert that democracy is an organization "originating in treachery, sustained by duplicity,
and in its development exhibiting multiform inconsist-
ency." Mr. Cadwalader and his party are welcome
to the benefits to be derived from all such slanderous
charges, and wholesale denunciations. It is quite
true that the American party has frequently suffered
by prominent democrats fastening themselves upon it,
as the contemptible and worthless sucking-fish does to
the whale, solely for the advantages to be derived from
the adhesion ; but it is not true that the democracy
rigorously exscinded such men from their organizations. Some of them, after having twice proved traitors ; first to the democratic and afterwards to the
American party, were received again by the former
with open arms and elevated to high positions of trust
and profit. The democratic ranks number many such
who are whigs, democrats, Americans, free-soilers,
abolitionists, or pro-slavery men, just as it suits their
convenience, or more especially, their interests. But
this furnishes no reason why we should denounce all
democrats, some of whom are as honourable men as
the country can boast, as traitors, tricksters, and
scoundrels. It is quite an easy thing to employ opprobrious epithets, and those who merit them most are
generally the aptest in their use. Who has not heard
the sootiest blackamoor taunt a mulatto with the

offensive name of " nigger ?" and it is quite an old
trick for an escaping pickpocket to divert attention
from himself by bawling out lustily in a crowd, " stop
thief ! stop thief !"

The declaration that there has existed or does exist
a fusion or alliance between the American party
and the Whigs is almost too ridiculous to deserve
notice. The author of the circular did not believe the
assertion. It is well known that the American associations embrace as many democrats as whigs, and
that their greatest strength is in old democratic districts. They have encountered quite as much hostility
from the whig as from the democratic party. And
instead of uniting with either of them, they have
repudiated the conduct of both, and preferred to maintain their identity and carry out their avowed principles independent of either. How is it with their
opponents ? These seem to have forgotten that they
ever possessed any principles to advocate, and show by
their recent conduct that the battles they have waged
against each other have been simply for the spoils of
office. In the early days of the Christian era, Herod
and Pilate united to put down the Redeemer. It was
rather an unholy alliance. So now the democrats and
whigs are affiliating to destroy their new and common
enemy. It does not require the gift of prophecy to
discern the result of this most singular warfare. In
a little while the whigs and democrats, who have
nothing to distinguish them but their names, will cease
to exist, and the political strife of the country will be
between two great parties, the American and the anti-

American. The former has already received large accessions from both the old organizations, and ere long will gather in all who are worth obtaining. The vituperations of its adversaries, instead of prolonging, are rapidly hastening, this consummation most devoutly to be wished. Mr. Cadwalader reiterates the old charge of riot and church-burning against the American party, and in so doing manifests but slight regard for his reputation for veracity. No man knows better than himself the injustice of this accusation. There is no fact in history more susceptible of the clearest proof than that the riots of 1844 were the work of the *democracy*. Irish Catholic democrats assailed meetings of American citizens lawfully and peaceably assembled; broke up those meetings; tore down the staging; and drove the speakers from the ground. Irish Catholic democrats fired balls and slugs from pistols and guns into crowds of American citizens who had met for the purpose of discussing the principles of their own government. Irish Catholic democrats brutally murdered in the streets of Philadelphia harmless men, for daring to exercise the right of freemen, in the expression of sentiments obnoxious to the democratic party. Irish Catholic democrats did everything in their power to provoke assaults upon their dwellings and churches. Irish Catholic democrats seriously regretted that their acts of violence were insufficient to incite the American party to retaliation, and, it was shrewdly suspected, had more to do than would be prudent to tell with the destruction of their religious edifices. Be this as it may, it is quite certain that they rejoiced in obtaining splendid new buildings, at the cost of the county, for the old ones that were destroyed.   And although every possible effort was made to that end, *not one member of the American party* was convicted of having any lot or part in the burning of Catholic churches.   On the contrary, it was proved beyond all question that the American party *protected the churches against provoked violence,* and prevented the destruction of many innocent lives by certain hot-brained democrats.   All this Mr. Cadwalader knew ; and yet he says, the American party "had become known by the opprobrious, but *well-deserved* name of ' church-burners.' "

It would be a great waste of time and paper to notice all the nonsense that Mr. Cadwalader has written to enlighten the people of Virginia in regard to the American party.   There are some things, however, in his precious circular sufficiently curious to merit preservation.   The writer has an admirable facility for blowing hot and cold with the same breath. In the paragraphs above quoted, it will be seen that he considers the know-nothing or American party, a mere fusion of the native American and whig parties. In that which follows, he ascribes the organization of the know-nothing party to democrats disaffected by the Catholic appointments of the president:

" An incident of the presidential election of 1852 had operated to make hostility to foreigners the pretext for subsequent anti-democratic organization. The president was from a state whose constitution is unfortunately disgraced by an intolerant

disfranchisement of those who profess the Catholic religion.
The orthodox democrats of that state, after a struggle to ex-
punge this illiberal clause from her constitution, had found the
local prejudice on the subject too strong to be overcome, and
had relinquished the endeavour in despair. During the elec-
tioneering canvass, an artful endeavour was made to excite
against him, on this account, the suspicion of the Catholic
population of the United States. This element of the democratic combination was thus rendered conspicuous. The party's
triumphant success in the presidential election was mainly due
to the concurrence of opinions in favour of the congressional
legislation of 1850, by which the constitutional rights of the
people of the slaveholding states had been maintained. But
the president, representing all those elements which had been
combined in this concurring support, was, on democratic
principles, under a necessity to distribute his executive patronage in such a manner as to give a just share to every one of
the various democratic interests which had been united in his
support. The Catholics received, therefore, a share of the patronage under circumstances which attracted particular attention. Disappointed expectants of office were consequently, in
some cases, easily inflamed into resentment at that part of the
distribution of patronage which had been beneficial to the
Catholics. Of this the former native American party took immediate advantage. The result was the organization of the
know-nothing order."

As allusion is obscurely made in the above para-
graph to a very interesting political fact, it may not
be amiss to make that fact a little more clear to those
who may not understand the particulars from the
language of the circular. Previous to the presidential
election of 1852, a democratic caucus of Pennsylvania
put forth the name of a gentleman for one of the most

responsible stations in the state, whom the democracy generally did not consider qualified for the position he sought; and so offensive was the nomination, that at the election, contrary to the usual custom, the masses of the party refused to support it, and in the county in which he lived, and where he was best known, the candidate run behind his ticket to an extent altogether unprecedented. The defeated candidate chanced to be a *Catholic*, and the Catholic democrats raised the hue and cry of religious proscription and intolerance, and not only maintained that their friend had been opposed on account of his faith, but required for him an appointment under the governor; and he consequently received the most desirable place in the state. Even this did not satisfy the demands of the Catholics; but on the accession of the present incumbent to the presidency, the defeated candidate was received into the cabinet as one of its members. This was effected, as Mr. Cadwalader says, "to give a just share to every one of the democratic interests which had been united in his (the president's) support,"—in other words, to conciliate the *Catholics* of the country, who *as Catholics* had entered the political arena, in the cause of the democracy. Instead of rebuking such an unrighteous combination, the president yielded to its demands. Honest religionists of other persuasions became alarmed, as well as thousands of good citizens who are connected with no regular church organizations. The greater portion of the democrats of the state considered the matter as a gross outrage. They

19

discovered that a single church party had more influence than the entire balance of the democracy combined. They did not attempt to conceal their just
indignation, and abandoned by thousands a party
which they could not otherwise regard than as danger-
ously corrupt. " The result was" *not* "the organization of the know-nothing order," but large accessions
to the American party, and the death-blow of democracy in Pennsylvania, as is shown by the last state
election. All that is said in the circular under consideration, about religious persecution, proscription
and intolerance, may go for what it is worth. It is
the special pleading of a lawyer, and will not have the
weight of a feather on an intelligent mind. Besides,
that subject has been placed in its proper light in other
portions of this book.

CHAPTER XXIII.

Mr. Cadwalader's circular, continued — Union of know-nothings and abolitionists — The American party independent of all factions — Immigration destructive of the interests of both the South and North by cheapening the price of labour — The dangerous dispositions of foreign settlers — Basis principles of the American party of Virginia.

THE attempt of Mr. Cadwalader to connect Americanism with abolitionism can be regarded as nothing better than an insult to the common sense of the slave-holding people of the south. In the following paragraphs there is scarcely a word of truth:

"This know-nothing agitation was a mere device of the opponents of democratic organization to carry the next presidential election by a combination of oppressors of our naturalized political brethren, with abolitionists and freesoilers. A pretext for the union of the know-nothing vote at the north with that of the abolition and freesoil factions, was, therefore, to be sought. It was found in the Nebraska bill.

"Whether the Nebraska bill was in itself right or wrong, availed nothing. It was made the pretext for a union of know-nothings and abolitionists in a crusade against all that was honest and conservative in the nation. Without such a combination, either the know-nothings or abolitionists, acting alone, would have been altogether powerless. At every state, county, and other municipal election since 1852, at which a formally established local democratic majority has been overcome at the north, the successful vote of our opponents has been the result of a secret combination of abolitionists and freesoilers, with

(219)

whigs, native Americans, and discontented outcasts of the democracy, united under the know-nothing organization.

" At the South, there was a stronger motive of secrecy in the attempted know-nothing organization. It was necessary there to conceal from all members of this Order the truth of that alliance with abolitionism and freesoilism, which was the local dependence of its northern members. Know-nothings of the north addressing themselves to the people of the slaveholding states, craftily suggested that comparatively few naturalized citizens had settled within their limits, and that this class of our citizens, preferring to reside at the north, or in the middle states, were generally freesoilers or abolitionists. They next urged, with hypocritical artifice, that a decrease of immigration would be consequent upon its discouragement, and that a repeal or modification of the naturalization laws would produce its discouragement, and thus tend to diminish the numbers of those hereafter aggregated in opposition to the constitutional rights of the slaveholder. The purpose of the shallow artifice was to create jealousies in which to sow the seeds of dissension between the people of the slaveholding states and the steadfast democratic supporters of their constitutional rights, who had hitherto not less been the steadfast supporters of the rights of the naturalized American. There never was a more deceptive pretence than that upon which this argument was presented to the people of the slaveholding states. A further motive of secrecy was found at the south, in an apprehension lest the proposition which they thus ventured to present in private, should be met in open discussion by men whose ability would enable them at once to encounter and refute it by demonstrating its sophistry.

" But the constitutional rights of the slaveholder have hitherto been maintained, and will in future be maintainable in the non-slaveholding states, under democratic organization alone. This organization, which, if sustained, will neither tolerate nor permit injustice to the slaveholder, as to these constitutional rights, will always extend an equally potent and effective protection to the naturalized American. The sure title of the one to this democratic protection is his unqualified concurrence in democratic protection of the other. The democracy, to sustain themselves, require, in return, the support of both. If, therefore the democracy, forsaken by the people of the slaveholding states, whom they have hitherto shielded from oppression, should find themselves unable to extend a sufficiently powerful protection to naturalized citizens, to prevent a repeal or modification of the naturalization laws, what would be the probable effects and consequences to the slaveholding states? The repeal of the Nebraska bill is now the pretext of its pretended opponents. Their hostility is really to the fugitive slave law. The real object of their combination with the know-nothings is its repeal. They forbear, as yet, to agitate the question openly, because when its agitation was attempted in 1852, the vote of twenty-seven of the thirty-one states, at the presidential election, showed the strength of the democracy with its legitimate supports of southern patriots on the one hand, upholding the rights of their naturalized brethren, and naturalized Americans, on the other hand, sustaining the constitutional rights of their southern fellow citizens. Our opponents hope, in dividing these forces, to conquer us. They know, that if either support were withdrawn, the force of the democracy aided only by the other, would be insufficient to resist their combination. Should it succeed, the fugitive slave law would be sacrificed as assuredly as the naturalization laws."

Now, in the name of common sense and good reason, what does all this balderdash mean? When and where has this amalgamation of know-nothings and freesoilers and abolitionists taken place? What have the principles of the American party to do with abolitionism on the one hand, or of slavery on the other? What especial bearing have they upon the interests of the freesoilers of the north or the slaveholders of the south? Had some rabid abolitionist of the north written to Mr.

19 *

Cadwalader to know whether or not Americanism was
intended to support the interests of southern pro-
slavery men, he would in all probability have written
as lengthy and wordy a circular to prove that the
know-nothing organization was intended to perpetuate
slavery, and extend the limits of the slave interests in
the yet unsettled territories.   Why did Mr. Orr write
to Mr. Cadwalader for information respecting a party
whose principles have never been hidden, but are proclaimed freely through the columns of a hundred independent journals, and as openly declared upon the
house-tops and at the corners of all the streets?   There
is not, nor has there ever been, any secrecy concerning these principles.   They have no especial bearing
on any local interests, north or south, east or west;
but aim to promote the welfare and prosperity of the
entire republic, and their beneficial influences will be
experienced in every section of the country, from the
northern limits of Maine to the southern extremity of
Louisiana; from the boisterous shores of the Atlantic
to the rock-bound coasts of the Pacific.   The American
party is the only political organization that, in its
operations, is calculated to benefit alike all classes of
American citizens and in all localities.   It has no
affinity with whiggery, democracy, freesoilism, abolitionism, or slavery.   It aims to promote the *general
good by general principles.*   What northern man is so
stupid as not to perceive that the immense immigration
of the lowest classes of Europeans is calculated to re-
duce the prices of labour, and bring to a level with
serfs, pæons, and slaves, the free labouring men of

America? What southerner so dull of comprehension as not to understand that the cheapening of free labour is destructive of the slaveholding interests? What man, northerner or southerner, cannot realize that any measures, intended and calculated to suppress the rapid influx of foreigners into the country, will tend to preserve and promote its general prosperity? Already is the labour of white immigrants in the north as cheap as that of negro labour in the south, and even in some of the slave states, the former has been placed in competition with the latter. Fanatical abolitionists may rejoice in this condition of things; for by encouraging it they are striking directly at the slaveholding interests. But the masses of the northern people,—the mechanics and working classes,—look on with alarm, and know that the same influences that abolitionists suppose will destroy the southern interests are alike destructive of their own. They are not blind to the fact, that the yearly immigration of thousands of hungry and naked free labourers must constantly decrease the demand for and price of free labour, and produce a corresponding decrease of their means of comfort and enjoyment. And hence, no question ever agitated the country, in which the people of the north and south had more cause to unite in political association. The only class of persons who have reason to apprehend the results of such a union, are aspirants and tricksters of the old organizations, who have made politics a trade, and are loth to lose the spoils of what has been a somewhat profitable employment.

Mr. Cadwalader unwittingly presents one of the

strongest reasons that can be given for the American movement, whilst threatening the southern people with its consequences.   He says:

" If the naturalization laws were altered through the slave-holding influence, what would be the consequences?   The government of the United States could not, under the constitution, prevent any present or future state of the Union from permitting at her pleasure unnaturalized residents to vote at all elections held within her limits, including those for presidential electors, and for members of Congress, and members of her own legislature.   Resident foreigners, therefore, would still be permitted thus to vote, as they now vote in several of the new states, and most, or all of the territories.   Unnaturalized foreigners would leave states, whose laws would locally disfranchise them, and go to states, or to territories, where they would be on a political equality with native citizens.   If there should be no such states, they would form, in the territorial wilderness, exclusive settlements of their own, to become hereafter states of our Union.   Their new political organizations, in sites where they might thus locate themselves, might, in various modes, if the feeling imputed to them existed, become practically dangerous to the slaveholding interest."

The writer is a short-sighted reasoner.   He here clearly shows the absolute necessity not only for the entire repeal of the naturalization laws, but the discouragement of immigration.   It was partly to avert the very evils he here predicts, that the American party was organized; and, to prevent the occurrence of such a state of affairs, every American, who values his country, should give it his countenance and support. Mr. Cadwalader, though ignorant of the subject he discusses, proves himself thoroughly acquainted with the spirit of the foreign population.   They are determined to have a hand in the government of our country; and if they are not permitted to manage matters their own way in one section, they will emigrate to another, where they will have less opposition to encounter. And if the southern people unite with their northern American brethren to curtail the privileges and lessen the influence of naturalized and unnaturalized foreigners, then they will avail themselves of whatever means and opportunities they can, to revenge themselves, by destroying, as far as it is possible, the slaveholder's interests. It was this spirit that incited the riots of 1844 in Philadelphia. And now the good people of the south are threatened with its consequences to be accomplished only by different means. We thank Mr. Cadwalader for this confession, and commend it to the serious consideration of all Americans.

As there is nothing further in the circular deserving of especial consideration, we shall close this chapter by giving Mr. Orr the information which he desires, and which Mr. Cadwalader has failed to communicate in the following

"BASIS PRINCIPLES OF THE AMERICAN PARTY OF VIRGINIA.

"Determined to preserve our political institutions in their original purity and vigour, and to keep them unadulterated and unimpaired by foreign influence, either civil or religious, as well as by home faction and home demagoguism; and believing that an American policy, religious, political, and commercial, is necessary for the attainment of these ends, we shall observe and carry out in practice, the following principles :

" 1. That the suffrages of the American people for political offices, should not be given to any other than those born on our soil, and reared and matured under the influence of our institutions.

" 2. That no foreigner ought to be allowed to exercise the elective franchise, till he shall have resided within the United States a sufficient length of time to enable him to become acquainted with the principles and imbued with the spirit of our institutions, and until he shall have become thoroughly identified with the great interests of our country.

" 3. That, whilst no obstacle should be interposed to the immigration of all foreigners of honest and industrious habits, and all privileges and immunities enjoyed by any native-born citizens of our country should be extended to all such immigrants, except that of participating in any of our political administrations ; yet all legal means should be adopted to obstruct and prevent the immigration of the vicious and worthless, the criminal and pauper.

" 4. That the *American* doctrine of religious toleration, and entire absence of all proscription for opinion's sake, should be cherished as one of the very fundamental principles of our civil freedom, and that any sect or party which believes and maintains that any foreign power, religious or political, has the right to control the conscience or direct the conduct of a freeman, occupies a position which is totally at war with the principles of freedom of opinion, and which is mischievous in its tendency, and which principle, if carried into practice, would prove wholly destructive of our religious and civil liberty.

" 5. That the Bible in the hands of every free citizen is the only permanent basis of all true liberty and genuine equality.

" 6. That the intelligence of the people is necessary to the right use and the continuance of our liberties, civil and religious; hence the propriety and importance of the promotion and fostering of all means of moral and intellectual culture by some adequate and permanent provision for general education.

"7. That the doctrine of availability, now so prevalent and controlling, in the nomination of candidates for office, in total disregard to all principles of right, of truth, and of justice, is essentially wrong, and should be by all good men condemned.

" 8. That, as a general rule, the same restrictions should be prescribed to the exercise of the power of removal from office, as are made necessary to be observed in the power of appointment thereto; and that executive influence and patronage should be scrupulously conferred and jealously guarded.

" 9. That the sovereignty of the states should be supreme in the exercise of all powers not expressly delegated to the federal government, and which may not be necessary and proper to carry out the powers so delegated, and that this principle should be observed and held sacred in all organizations of the American party.

" 10. That all sectarian intermeddling with politics

or political institutions, coming from whatever source it may, should be promptly resisted by all such means as seem to be necessary and proper for this end.

"11. That whilst the perpetuity of the present form of the federal government of the United States is actually necessary for the proper development of all the resources of this country, yet the principle of non-intervention, both on the part of the federal government and of the several states of the union, in the municipal affairs of each other, is essential to the peace and prosperity of our country, and to the well-being and permanence of our institutions, and at the same time the only reliable bond of brotherhood and union.

"12. The red republicanism and licentious indulgence in the enjoyment of civil privileges, are as much to be feared and deprecated by all friends to well-regulated government and true liberty, as any of the forms of monarchy and despotism.

"13. That the true interests and welfare of this country, the honour of this nation, the individual and private rights of its citizens, conspire to demand that all other questions arising from party organizations, or from any other source, should be held subordinate to and in practice made to yield to the great principles herein promulgated."

APPENDIX.

THE NATIONAL CONVENTION.

THE first National Convention of the American party was held on the 5th and 7th of July, 1845, at Philadelphia, in the Assembly Buildings, corner of Tenth and Chestnut streets. Delegates, whose names are given below, were present from fourteen states, viz. Pennsylvania, Massachusetts, New York, New Jersey, Delaware, Kentucky, Ohio, Missouri, Mississippi, Georgia, New Hampshire, Vermont, Indiana, and North Carolina. The officers of the convention were

President—H. A. S. Dearborne, Mass.

Vice Presidents—L. D. Chapin, N. Y.; Charles Sexton, N. J.; Thomas P. Grover, Pa.; William N. Haldeman, Ky.; Joseph K. Burtis, Mo.

Secretaries—W. L. Prall, N. Y.; Edwin R. Campbell, O.; John F. Driggs, N. Y.; George G. West, Pa.

The following Address to the Citizens of the United States was unanimously adopted, and ordered to be published:

20   (229)

ᵉ6666666

ADDRESS OF THE NATIONAL CONVENTION.

FELLOW CITIZENS:—When, in the history of nations, great and increasing evils arise, and invade the rights or threaten to destroy the just and natural privileges of a people, it becomes equally the duty and the interest of that people to present to the world such representation of their grievances as shall tend to justify their efforts to remove those evils, and establish permanent means to prevent their recurrence. It has been the fate of all nations, and especially of republics, to suffer, in various ways, from the encroachments and assumptions of a foreign people; and it is an unerring truth of history, that most of them have lost their liberty and power by such means. The peculiar institutions of the United States have exposed them more than any other, to the evils and wrongs of foreign encroachments; and experience has already shown that they, like most other people of historical notice, are now realizing like consequences from like causes. Influenced by these considerations, a large portion of the native citizens of these United States have felt it to be their most solemn and imperative duty, to associate and pledge themselves one to another, for the purpose of awakening their countrymen to a sense of the evils already experienced from foreign intrusion and usurpation, and the imminent danger to which all they love and venerate, as native Americans, is momentarily exposed from foreign influence; and also to use all honourable means to diminish those evils, and oppose barriers to their future progress. They have therefore called together, in convention, in the city of Philadelphia, the representatives of those native Americans who, clearly seeing and feeling the evils and dangers complained of, have the moral courage to oppose and redress them; and now, in conformity with usage and duty, these representatives announce to their associates and their fellow citizens, the great objects contemplated by the native American party, their reasons for action, and the principles by which they propose hereafter to be governed.

DECLARATION.

We, the delegates elect, to the first National Convention of the native American body of the United States of America, assembled at Philadelphia, on the 4th day of July, 1845, for the purpose of devising a plan of concerted political action in defence of American institutions against the encroachments of foreign influence, open or concealed, hereby, solemnly, and before Almighty God, make known to our fellow-citizens, our country, and the world, the following incontrovertible facts, and the course of conduct consequent thereon, to which, in duty to the cause of human rights, and the claims of our beloved country, we mutually pledge our lives, our fortunes, and our sacred honour.

The danger of foreign influence, threatening the gradual destruction of our national institutions, failed not to arrest the attention of the Father of his country,

in the very dawn of American liberty. Not only its
direct agency in rendering the American system liable
to the poisonous influence of European policy—a
policy at war with the fundamental principles of the
American constitution—but also its still more fatal
operation in aggravating the virulence of partisan
warfare—has awakened deep alarm in the mind of
every intelligent patriot, from the days of Washington
to the present time.

The influx of a foreign population, permitted, after
little more than a nominal residence, to participate in
the legislation of the country, and the sacred right of
suffrage, produced comparatively little evil during the
earlier years of the republic; for that influx was then
limited by the considerable expenses of a transatlantic
voyage, by the existence of many wholesome restraints
upon the acquisition of political prerogatives, by the
constant exhaustion of the European population in
long and bloody continental wars, and by the slender
inducements offered for emigration to a young and
sparsely peopled country, contending for existence
with a boundless wilderness, inhabited by savage men.
Evils which are only prospective, rarely attract the
notice of the masses, and, until peculiar changes were
effected in the political condition of Europe, the increased facilities for transportation, and the madness
of partisan legislation in removing all effective guards
against the open prostitution of the right of citizenship, had converted the slender current of naturalization into a torrent threatening to overwhelm the influence of the natives of the land; the far-seeing

vision of the statesman, only, being fixed upon the distant, but steadily approaching cloud.

But, since the barriers against the improper extension of the right of suffrage were bodily broken down, for a partisan purpose, by the Congress of 1825, the rapidly increasing numbers and unblushing insolence of the foreign population of the worst classes, have caused the general agitation of the question, *"How shall the institutions of the country be preserved from the blight of foreign influence, insanely legalized through the conflicts of domestic parties?"* Associations, under different names, have been formed by our fellow-citizens, in many states of this confederation, from Louisiana to Maine, all designed to check this imminent danger before it becomes irremediable, and, at length, a National Convention of the great American people, born upon the soil of Washington, has assembled to digest, suggest, and announce a plan of operations, by which the grievances of an abused hospitality, and the consequent degradation of political morals, may be redressed, and the tottering columns of the temple of Republican Liberty secured upon the sure foundation of an enlightened nationality.

In calling for support upon every American who loves his country pre-eminently, and every adopted citizen of moral and intellectual worth, who would secure to his compatriots yet to come amongst us, the blessings of political protection, the safety of person and property, it is right that we should make known the grievances which we propose to redress, and the

20*

manner in which we shall endeavour to effect our
object.

It is an incontrovertible truth, that the civil institutions of the United States of America have been
seriously affected, and that they now stand in imminent
peril from the rapid and enormous increase of the
body of residents of foreign birth, imbued with foreign
feelings, and of an ignorant and immoral character,
who receive, under the present lax and unreasonable
laws of naturalization, the elective franchise and the
right of eligibility to political office.

The whole body of foreign citizens, invited to our
shores under a constitutional provision adapted to
other times and other political conditions of the world,
and of our country especially, has been endowed by
American hospitality with gratuitous privileges unnecessary to the enjoyment of those inalienable rights
of man—*life, liberty, and the pursuit of happiness*—
privileges wisely reserved to the natives of the soil, by
the governments of all other civilized nations. But,
familiarized by habit with the exercise of these indul-
gences, and emboldened by increasing numbers, a vast
majority of those who constitute this foreign body,
now claim as an original right, that which has been
so incautiously granted as a favour,—thus attempting
to render inevitable the prospective action of laws
adopted upon a principle of mere expediency, made
variable at the will of Congress, by the express terms
of the Constitution, and heretofore repeatedly revised
to meet the exigencies of the times.

In former years, this body was recruited chiefly

from the victims of political oppression, or the active
and intelligent mercantile adventurers of other lands;
and it then constituted a slender representation of
the best classes of the foreign population, well fitted
to add strength to the state, and capable of being
readily educated in the peculiarly American science
of political self-government. Moreover, while wel-
coming the stranger of every condition, our laws then
wisely demanded of every foreign aspirant for political
rights, *a certificate of practical good citizenship.* Such
a class of aliens were followed by no foreign demagogues, they were courted by no domestic demagogues,
they were purchased by no parties, they were de-
bauched by no emissaries of kings. A wall of fire
separated them from such a baneful influence, erected
by their intelligence, their knowledge, their virtue and
love of freedom. But for the last twenty years, the
road to civil preferment and participation in the legislative and executive government of the land has been
laid broadly open, alike to the ignorant, the vicious,
and the criminal; and a large proportion of the foreign
body of citizens and voters now constitutes a representation of the worst and most degraded of the European
population, victims of social oppression, of personal
vices, utterly divested by ignorance or crime, of the
moral and intellectual requisites for political self-
government.

Thus tempted by the suicidal policy of these United
States, and favoured by the facilities resulting from
the modern improvements of navigation, numerous
societies and corporate bodies in foreign countries

have found it economical to transport to our shores, at public and private expense, the feeble, the imbecile, the idle, and intractable, thus relieving themselves of the burdens resulting from the vices of the European social systems, by availing themselves of the generous errors of our own.

The almshouses of Europe are emptied upon our coast, *and this by our own invitation*, not casually or to a trivial extent, but systematically, and upon a constantly increasing scale. The bedlams of the old world have contributed their share to the torrent of immigration, and the lives of our citizens have been attempted in the streets of our capital cities by madmen, just liberated from European hospitals upon the express condition that they should be transported to America. By the orders of European governments the punishment of crimes has been commuted for banishment to the land of the free; and criminals in irons have crossed the ocean, to be cast loose upon society on their arrival upon our shores. The United States are rapidly becoming the lazar house and penal colony of Europe; nor can we reasonably censure such proceedings; they are legitimate consequences of our own unlimited benevolence; and it is of such material that we profess to manufacture free and enlightened citizens by a process occupying five short years at most, but practically oftentimes embraced in a much shorter period of time.

The mass of immigrants, formerly cast among the natives of the soil, has increased from the ratio of 1 in 40 to that of 1 in 7! a like advance in 15 years will leave the natives of the soil in a minority in their own land! Thirty years ago these strangers came by units and tens, now they swarm by thousands. (It is estimated that 300,000 will arrive within the present year.) Formerly, most of them sought only for an honest livelihood and a provision for their families, and rarely meddled with those institutions of which it was impossible they could comprehend the nature; *now* each new comer seeks political preferment, and struggles to fasten on the public purse with an avidity in strict proportion to his ignorance and unworthiness of public trust,—having been SENT for the purpose of obtaining political ascendancy in the government of the nation, having been SENT to exalt their allies to power, having been SENT to work a revolution from republican freedom to the divine rights of monarchs.

From these unhappy circumstances has arisen an *imperium in imperio*, a body uninformed and vicious, foreign in feeling, prejudice, and manner, yet armed with a vast and often a controlling influence over the policy of a nation whose benevolence it abuses, and whose kindness it habitually insults; a body as dangerous to the rights of the intelligent foreigner, and to the prospect of its own immediate progeny, as it is threatening to the liberties of the country, and the hopes of rational freedom throughout the world; a body ever ready to complicate our foreign relations by embroiling us with the hereditary hates and feuds of other lands, and to disturb our domestic peace by its crude ideas, mistaking license for liberty, and the overthrow of individual rights for republican political equality: a body ever the ready tool of foreign and domestic demagogues, and steadily endeavouring by misrule to establish popular tyranny under a cloak of false democracy. Americans, false to their country, and led on to moral crime by the desire of dishonest gain, have scattered their agents over Europe, inducing the malcontent and the unthrifty to exchange a life of compulsory labour in foreign lands, for relative comfort, to be maintained by the tax-paying industry of our overburdened and deeply indebted community.

Not content with the usual and less objectionable licenses of trade, these fraudulent dealers habitually deceive a worthier class of victims, by false promises of employment, and assist in thronging the already crowded avenues of simple labour with a host of competitors, whose first acquaintance with American faith springs from a gross imposture, and whose first feeling on discovering the cheat, is reasonable mistrust, if not implacable revenge. The importation of the physical necessities of life may be burdened with duties, which many deem extravagant; but the importation of vice and idleness—of seditious citizens and factious rulers —is not only unrestricted by anything beyond a nominal tax, but is actually encouraged by a system which transforms the great patrimony of the nation, purchased by the blood of our fathers, into a source of bounty for the promotion of immigration.

Whenever an attempt is made to restrain this fatal evil, the native and adopted demagogues protest against an effort which threatens to deprive them of their most important tools; and such is the existing organization of our established political parties, that should either of them essay the reform of an abuse which both acknowledge to be fraught with ruin, that party sinks, upon the instant, into a minority, divested of control and incapable of result.

From such causes has been derived a body, armed with political power, in a country of whose system it is ignorant, and in whose institutions it feels little interest, except for the purpose of personal advancement.

This body has formed and encouraged associations under *foreign names*, to promote measures of foreign policy, and to perpetuate foreign clannishness among adopted citizens of the United States; in contravention of that spirit of union and nationality, without which no people can legitimately claim a place among the nations of the earth.

It has employed the power of associations to embroil the people of this country in the political disputes of other lands, with which the United States are anxious to encourage peace and amity.

It has introduced *foreign emblems*, not only of national, but of partisan character, in the civic processions and public displays of bodies of men, claiming the title of American citizens and sworn to American fealty; by which means it has fomented frequent riot and murder.

It has adopted national costumes and national insignia *foreign to the country*, in arming and equipping military corps, constituting a part of the national guard, with its word of command in a foreign language,

in open defiance of our military code, by which means
it has weakened the discipline of the militia, and rendered it less available for defence in time of war.

It has entered into the strife of parties as a separate
organization, unknown to the laws, suffering itself to
be addressed and led to the contest—not as a portion
of the great American family of freemen, but combined
as *foreigners;* thus virtually falsifying its oaths of
allegiance, and proving beyond denial, its entire unfit-
ness for political trust.

It has formed and encouraged political combinations,
holding the balance of power between opposing parties,
which combinations have offered their votes and influence to the highest bidder in exchange for pledges of
official position and patronage.

It has boasted of giving governors to our states, and
chief magistrates to the nation.

By serving as an unquestioning and uncompromising tool of executive power, it has favoured a political
centralism, hostile to the rights of the independent
states, and the sovereignty of the people.

It has facilitated the assumption by the national
executive, of the right to remove from office, *without
the consent of the Senate*, persons who only can be
appointed *with such consent;* which assumption is an
obvious evasion of the spirit of the constitution.

It has encouraged political combinations for the purpose of effecting sectarian measures, in defiance of the
fundamental law of the United States, and the consti-
tutions of the states in which such efforts have been
made.

It has given rise to the organization and arming of *foreign bands*, leagued for the purpose of controlling the freedom of discussion and opposing the constitutional assembling of American freemen, seeking the redress of political grievances, which lawless bands have repeatedly threatened, assaulted, and temporarily dispersed, lawful political meetings of native citizens, in various places.

Emboldened by the often-tested weakness of the constituted authorities, resulting, as we solemnly believe, from the ascendancy of the foreign influence at the polls, a host of these foreign assassins at length proceeded to redden the gutters of the second city of the Union with the blood of unarmed native citizens, without even the semblance of provocation, and with the avowed determination to prevent any political assemblage of the natives of the soil within the limits of one of the political divisions of a sovereign American state.

Prostrated in this attempt by the ungovernable fury of an outraged community, moving in mass, to avenge such insult to the flag of their country, trampled and torn beneath the feet of the very refuse of Europe— these lawless bands and their abettors have since fomented extensive riot and open insurrection; and, uniting with their prejudiced fellow-countrymen, together with domestic demagogues of various political creeds, have striven unceasingly, to fasten upon the victims of their treasonable and murderous proceedings, the odium of crimes originating with themselves;—thus exciting bloody contest between opposing bodies of

21

native citizens, impairing, by division, the remaining
political influence of the native population, and weak-
ening the bonds of social harmony, and the obligation
of the laws.   Collision of opinion has thus been followed by collision of arms in deadly array, in the very
sanctuary of our freedom, by the myrmidons of the
crowned heads of Europe.   If this double struggle,
and aggravated danger, *does not constitute a crisis of
national emergency*, we are yet to learn, what combination of power inimical to liberty, can endanger the
republic, or peril the permanence of our institutions.

The body of adopted citizens with foreign interests
and prejudices, is annually advancing with rapid
strides, in geometrical progression.   Already it has
acquired a control over our elections, which cannot be
entirely corrected, even by the wisest legislation, until
the present generation shall be numbered with the
past.   Already it has notoriously swayed the course
of national legislation, and invaded the purity of local
justice.   In a few years its unchecked progress would
cause it to outnumber the native defenders of our
rights, and would then inevitably dispossess *our* off-
spring and its own of the inheritance for which *our
fathers bled*, or plunge this land of happiness and
peace into the horrors of civil war.

The correction of these evils can never be effected
by any combination governed by the tactics of other
existing parties.

If either of the old parties as such, were to attempt
an extension of the term of naturalization (from five
to twenty-one years), it would be impossible for it to

carry out the measure, because it would immediately
be abandoned by the foreign voters. This great measure can be carried out only by an organization like
our own, made up of those who have given up their
former political preferences.

For these reasons, we recommend the immediate
organization of the truly patriotic native citizens
throughout the United States, for the purpose of re-
sisting the progress of foreign influence in the conduct
of American affairs, and the correction of such political abuses as have resulted from unguarded or partisan legislation on the subject of naturalization, so far
as these abuses admit of remedy without encroachment
upon the vested rights of foreigners, who have been
already legally adopted into the bosom of the nation;
and in furtherance of this object, we present the public
with the following statement of the political principles
and objects of the native American body, whose duly
constituted representatives we are.

PRINCIPLES.

WE hold that, with few exceptions, no man, educated
under one system of government, can ever become
thoroughly imbued with the essence and spirit of another
system essentially different in character.

That no man can eradicate, entirely, the prejudices
and attachments associated with the land of his birth,
so as to become a perfectly safe depositary for political trust, in any other country.

That the obligation of an oath of fealty to a foreign nation has been decided, by every civilized nation but our own, to be of secondary power, when brought into collision with the natural fealty due to the native land. And, although we have as yet no decision of this question in our own supreme court, all precedents bearing on the subject lead us to anticipate a similar conclusion there.

And, therefore, that the elective franchise, which is the primary and fundamental element of popular sovereignty, can only be entirely secure when held exclusively in the hands of natives of the soil.

But, in consideration of the present and previous policy of our government, we are willing, at present, to extend, as a boon, to all peaceful and well-disposed strangers hereafter settling among us, not only every security enjoyed by the native in the protection of person, property, and the legal pursuit of happiness, but also the right of suffrage, UPON THE SAME TERMS AS THOSE IMPOSED UPON THE NATIVES, namely a legally authenticated residence of at least twenty-one years within the limits of the country.

We advocate such an amendment to the constitution of the United States, as may be necessary to preclude the votes of persons not legally citizens of the United States, in the choice of national representatives or delegates from the several states and territories.

We stand pledged, in the exercise of our constitutional right of selecting those candidates for office whom we esteem most capable and best informed, to confine our political nominations to the American born

citizens of the United States, including such foreign
born citizens only, as may have been parties to the
federal constitution at the time of its adoption.

We solemnly protest against all intermingling of
national policy with the local policy of particular
states, on questions involving the reserved rights of
those states.

We hold that all minor questions of expediency in
legislating upon subjects unconnected with the fundamental structure of the government; such as fiscal
and commercial regulations, the management of the
public domain, and the proceeds therefrom, &c., belong,
by right, to the representatives of the people, and
those of the several states, to be by them discussed
and decided, from time to time, after mature argument, under the constitutional responsibility of those
public agents, each to his own proper constituency
and to the country; and that the adoption of any
previous test or determination upon such questions by
any national party, degrades it into a *faction*, and by
leading to final decision before argument obstructs the
course of rational legislation. If it be asked what
measures of public import we most favour, as a party,
we answer, all that stand high as American measures,
in contradistinction to foreign. Native agriculture
we cherish first; native industry, first and last, in
every branch of trade, art, ingenuity, mechanics, and
invention. We aim at the independence of our country
in all things, moral, intellectual, physical, and political—in works of the hand as well as in works of the
head, in manual labour and in mental sagacity. We

21 *

desire to make our government what our fathers designed it should be, and witness native statesmen in power, native industry triumphant over foreign labour, and native hearts announcing America emancipated from all the world.

We advocate such an amendment of the constitution of the United States as shall reconcile its letter with its spirit, on the subject of executive appointments, rendering all officers commissioned by and with the consent of *the senate*, incapable of removal, except by and with the like consent.

We recommend to the native Americans of the several states, a prompt resistance to all sectarian intermeddling with politics or political institutions, come from what source soever it may; the absolute freedom of religious opinion being the corner-stone of American civilization.

We also recommend to the native Americans of the several states the careful fostering and improvement of local institutions for public instruction, to be supported at the public expense, without which, a government of the people must speedily become a government of ignorance and probable depravity.

We also recommend to the native Americans of the several states, in their systems of education, a full recognition of the Bible, as Divine authority for the rights of man, as well as for the separation of church and state, on which depends so essentially the pursuit of happiness and freedom of conscience. To the Bible we are indebted for the wand that broke the sceptre of tyrants, and crumbled to atoms the church and

state despotisms of those potentates, who associate
religion with their political systems; who degrade the
people in order to rule them, and interdict education
and knowledge among the masses, lest intelligence
should inform them of their rights, instruct them how
to break asunder their bonds, and rise to the true
dignity of God-created freedom. When the ambition
of kings projected the slavery of the people, they
locked up the Bible, and invested themselves with the
attributes of divinity. A divine right to enslave was
admitted when the human right was denied. Hence,
in all arbitrary governments, the state is incorporated
with the church, under the monstrous paradox that
man, in the possession of his natural rights, is incompetent to self-government. The reading of the
Bible among the people exploded this doctrine, and
the native Americans defend it, and will continue
to defend it, against all foreign aggression, as necessary to freedom of conscience, and the equal rights
of man.

Having thus completed an outline of the principles
and policy advocated by the native American political
party, as a national party, we call upon every true
friend of his country to rally under our standard,
before it becomes too late; we invite the assistance of
every adopted citizen of sufficient intelligence to perceive his own real interest, and that of his posterity.
Warring with no particular sect, attacking no particular nation, regardless of the spleen of pre-existing
parties, we are gathering to the combat in opposition
to that foreign influence, and those abuses of party

spirit, which were so ably foretold by Washington and Jefferson. Invoking Heaven in testimony of the purity of our motives, we have solemnly determined never to relax our efforts until the Star-Spangled Banner floats freely over the renationalized land of our birth and our affections.

RESOLUTIONS.

Believing our free institutions, if worth anything, *to be worth preserving*, and transmitting *unimpaired:*

Believing the *permanency* of those institutions to depend upon the *honest* and *intelligent* exercise of the right of suffrage:

Believing that ruin, if it come, will come through a *perversion* and *abuse* of that right:

Believing such perversion and abuse to have already prevailed, and to be now increasing, to an alarming extent:

Believing that the greatest source of evil, in this respect, is to be found in the rapid influx of ignorant foreigners, and the facility with which they are converted into citizens:

Believing that Americans in *form* should, and of right, ought to be, Americans at *heart:*

Believing that, under any circumstances, it is dangerous to commit the ballot-box, *the Ark of our Freedom's Covenant*, to foreign hands, or submit our destinies to the possible control of them who may be foreigners in *heart*, and American in *form* only:

Believing that, from any of the old political organizations as such, we cannot hope for any radical reform of the evils we deprecate :

Therefore, *Resolved*, That we do hereby form ourselves into a national political party, for the radical reform of abuses, and the preservation of our institutions and our liberties, under the name of the Native American Party.

Resolved, That, as native Americans, we cannot consent to give our political suffrages to any other than to those born on our soil and matured among our institutions.

Resolved, That no foreigner, hereafter coming to these United States, shall be allowed to exercise the elective franchise, until he shall have been a resident here *at least* twenty-one years.

Resolved, That while every constitutional effort should be made to guard against the deleterious consequences of a rapidly increasing immigration, by the enactment of the most efficient laws for the accomplishment of that all-important object, still a generous magnanimity requires that those aliens who are, or may become, inhabitants of the United States, should be kindly received, and every privilege extended to them, except that of participating in any of our political administrations, and exercising the right of suffrage, until after a residence of at least twenty-one years.

Resolved, That, as native Americans, we will foster and defend all the great interests of our country, its agriculture, its commerce, its mechanics and fine arts, manufactures, navigation, mining, and science and literature, against the world.

Resolved, That we urge the promotion and fostering of all means of moral and intellectual culture by permanent provisions for general education, believing the intelligence of the people to be necessary to the right use and the permanence of our liberties, civil and religious.

Resolved, That we advocate the universal toleration of every religious faith and sect, and the total separation of all sectarianism and politics.

Resolved, That the Bible, as the only basis of pure Christianity, lies at the bottom of all true liberty and equality, and thus, as the corner-stone of our free institutions, should be freely read by all men.

Resolved, That removals from important offices under the general government, should be made, like appointments, by and with the advice and consent of the senate, or other approving body, except in the absence of the senate, when the president may have the power to suspend *for cause.*

Resolved, That these principles, lying as they do, at the very foundation of our political freedom, and even existence, involve, and are paramount to all others, however important to our external prosperity.

Resolved, That the interest, the real welfare of all parties, the honour of the nation, all require that subordinate party questions should be made to yield to the great principles for which we are contending.

Resolved, That organizations of native American

associations should be established in all our towns and wards of cities.

Resolved, That the appointment of two delegates from each congressional district, be recommended to meet in general convention on the second Tuesday of May, 1847, to nominate candidates for president and vice president of the United States, and that the place of meeting be Pittsburgh, Pa.

Resolved, That the native American party do and will advocate the principle, that the naturalization of foreigners be confined exclusively to the courts of the United States, and that a public registration of all applicants for the elective franchise be made.

Resolved, That we advocate the principle, that no alien shall be naturalized, except on the production of a custom-house certificate, to be procured on his landing on these American shores, proving his residence of twenty-one years; such certificate to be given up to be cancelled.

Resolved, That we hold it to be the duty of all true native Americans, to give their suffrages to those only who subscribe heartily to our principles, and will maintain them.

Resolved, That we do advocate the passage of laws imposing upon all foreigners coming hither for purposes of permanent residence, a capitation tax, sufficiently large to prevent the excessive influx of the vicious and pauper immigrants, and that we do it as a matter of self-defence.

Resolved, That, as native Americans, we hold it to be our duty to take high moral ground on all subjects, to grapple with the principles of right, of truth, and of justice, without regard to mere questions of availability, and to contend for them fearlessly against the world.

Resolved, That we recommend that no alien be permitted to land in these United States, without a certificate of good moral character, and who is able to provide for his own support, which certificate shall be signed by the United States consul of the port from whence he sailed, in conformity with the act of Congress, passed in 1802, under President Jefferson.

Resolved, That the several executive committees of the states be requested to appoint each two proper persons, to constitute a corresponding national committee.

DELEGATES.

L. C. Levin,	Jeremiah E. Eldridge,
Thomas D. Grover,	Charles Perley,
Joseph B. Strafford,	Minard Lefevre,
Peter Sken Smith,	Thomas Winship,
L. M. Troutman,	Jacob Townsend,
Richard W. Green,	Benjamin C. Dutcher,
George W. Reed,	Daniel G. Taylor,
Amos Phillips,	Lewis Blanche,
Samuel B. Lewis,	Thomas H. Oakley,
Samuel H. Norton,	Charles Devoe,
P. B. Carter,	William Steele,
E. J. Sneeder,	E. C. Blake,
David Bricker,	William Leaycraft,
M. W. May,	John Young,

Jacob Lansing,
Rawson Harmon,
Charles Knight,
J. F. Whitney,
J. Q. Kettelle,
J. W. Monroe,
L. H. Braley,
A. D. Stiles,
Charles Ruggles,
J. L. Moore,
Lora Nash,
John A. King,
Aaron D. Thompson,
John Lloyd,
Charles M. Brown,
George F. Penrose,
Stephen Reed,
Charles D. Brown,
John Arnold,
George G. Maris,
Leander N. Ott,
Wm. Duncan,
George Everson,
E. Jackson,
Edward Griffins,
Jacob Weaver,
Thomas Ford,
O. C. Lombard,
Jesse Mann,
F. C. Messenger,
George Emerson,

H. A. S. Dearborne,
L. B. Bodge,
J. B. Robinson,
Franklin Ferguson,
Dr. J. Symmes,
Jesse Ford,
John Johnson,
Edward R. Campbell,
James H. Burtis,
H. H. Tucker,
G. W. Hartshorne,
George G. West,
John Allen,
Thomas Wattson,
J. W. Ashmead,
E. W. Keyser,
W. D. Baker,
Oliver P. Cornman,
Wm. M. Evans,
Wm. McCormick,
John F. Driggs,
Edward Green,
William Forbes,
W. L. Prall,
James Griffiths,
Thomas Hogan,
Peter Squiers,
Dr. D. C. Freeman,
W. C. Dusenbery,
Charles Alden,
Isaac S. Smith,

22

William R. Wagstaff,
Edward Harte,
Philip Jordan,
Wm. Taylor,
C. J. Fountain,
Samuel Gage,
John Locher,
Thomas R. Whitney,
Frederick H. Way,
Joseph Hufty,
S. G. Steele,
Loring D. Chapin,
William Kirpt,
John Mount,
George Youngs,
James Covel, Sr.,
Robert H. Golder,
William W. Wetmore,
Purdon Lapham,
William Bennett,
Elijah K. Wilds,
John F. Vanlear,
Jacob Teese,
George Ford,
Kirkpatrick Ewing,
E. C. Reigart,

Alex. M. Kenney,
George W. Twining,
Daniel Kendig,
Archibald Reeves,
Benjamin R. Snider,
Jos. Allison,
James Sturgis,
Samuel B. Lewis,
A. B. Ely,
Richard L. Wykoff,
Willis Ames,
James McDonald,
John Skillman, Jr.,
Morgan Everson,
Robert C. Russell,
Evan Smith,
Nathan'l Holmes, Jr.,
Chas. Sexton,
Albert Thatcher,
Thomas McCorkel,
W. N. Haldeman,
James G. Caldwell,
Hector Orr,
W. H. Farrar,
J. Hepherd.

FOUNDERS OF THE AMERICAN PARTY.

THE following list embraces the names of many of the original and most prominent members of the American party in Philadelphia. It is necessarily imperfect; but many names now omitted will be inserted in a subsequent edition.

Ackney, G. W.
Addicks, John E.
Addis, Charles
Addis, John
Afflick, Morris
Albright, Peter
Allen, John
Allison, Joseph
Alter, Jacob
Amer, Joseph H.
Anderson, John
App, George
Ardis, Wright B.
Arns, James R.
Arrison, Henry D.
Artkens, Charles C.
Ashhurst, Lewis R.
Ashmead, Charles W.
Ashmead, J. B.
Ashmead, John W.
Ashmead, L. R.
Ashmead, Samuel
Atkinson, Samuel C.
Awll, Charles W.
Baker, George
Baker, William D.
Baker, J. G.

Ballantine, Thomas
Banning, William L.
Bardin, A. Z.
Barnes, William D.
Barncastle, John
Barona, N. T.
Barrett, C. B.
Bartlett, George
Bartram, John W.
Bayne, John D.
Beard, David A.
Beck, William
Beck, John A.
Beisel, Simon
Berriman, M. W.
Beryon, R. G.
Bethell, Joshua
Betton, Thomas F.
Beckendach, John
Bird, S. D.
Bird, Thomas
Bishop, Joseph
Brick, Samuel R.
Bill, Henry
Bingham, John
Birkey, William J. A.
Blunden, William

Bonsall, James S.
Bonsall, E. C.
Bodine, Samuel T.
Bolton, William P.
Bonnell, Samuel
Boileau, Isaac B.
Book, Harman
Booth, Edwin
Boshart, J.
Bockius, George
Bockius, John C.
Boucher, Joseph
Bouvier, Peter
Brady, A.
Bradford, John O.
Brewster, Joseph S.
Brewster, Thomas
Brenizer, Amos E.
Brown, Robert
Brodhead, John
Brewster, Edmund
Brooks, Henry B.
Broome, Jacob
Brunson, Charles F.
Bryan, Isaiah
Bryant, John H.
Busby, Hezekiah
Byerly, John
Campbell, F. H.
Campbell, James A. A.
Campbell, Jos. M.
Campbell, J. H.

Carter, William J.
Carter, P. B.
Carpenter, Charles
Carrigan, Jacob
Carroll, Charles W.
Catlin, James C.
Cassidy, Thomas M.
Chambers, J. S.
Chase, Edwin T.
Chase, Heber
Chambers, James
Chaloner, A. D.
Christine, Thomas
Chulston, William K.
Clother, Thomas
Clouds, James
Clouser, William
Claghorn, John W.
Clark, John
Clarke, William M.
Clandamer, J. M.
Clement, Henry A.
Coane, Robert
Colon, J. R.
Colton, David
Copper, John C.
Cooper, William
Cooper, J. B.
Comegys, B. B.
Cooley, A. B.
Cooke, Thomas
Coyle, A. C.

Copeland, William

Coleman, Jacob

Conrad, David

Conrow, W. G.

Coates, Reynell

Cornman, Oliver P.

Colon, J. R.

Cox, Charles D.

Cramp, William

Crap, George M.

Craven, D. C.

Craig, William

Crout, Henry

Danenhower, Wm. W.

Dale, William H.

Davies, John

David, E. M.

Daniels, Geo. W.

Davis, William

Dacosta, John C.

Dearry, Thos.

Dehart, Abraham

Deas, James H.

Dearr, H.

De Groat, S. M.

De Hart, Abraham

Dickerson, Wm. R.

Dobbs, John

Dock, Jacob

Dobleman, John C.

Dolby, John

Deller, Adam

Dubosq, Philip L.

Dubosq, George

Duncan, Jas. J.

Duncan, A. C.

Durfor, F.

Dunton, Isaac

Dych, J.

Edwin, Alfred

Einwechter, Henry

Elliott, H. H. K.

Elliott, J. L.

Ellis, C. W.

Elliott, J.

Elder, Henry G.

Elmer, Alexander

Elmes, C. H.

Elmes, H. S.

Emerick, George

Erben, H. S.

Esher, William

Etter, David

Everhaur, Wm.

Evans, Randolph

Evans, Josiah

Evans, Wm. M.

Fairchild, Wm. L.

Faunce, Michael

Faunce, William

Fisher, John

Fithian, George

22 *

Fisher, S. H.

Flinn, John

Fletcher, Joshua A.

Flegal, John G.

Floyd, Jas.

Floyd, John

Fœring, A.

Fortner, C.

Fox, J. D.

Friend, John

Fritz, Peter

Freheller, Wm. H.

Frost, C. K.

Franks, W. D.

Franks, Henry D.

Fulton, Wm. H.

Gardy, Joseph

Gaskell, Benj.

Gaskell, Edward

George, D. D.

Gemeny, A. R.

Germon, John S.

Gihon, James L.

Gihon, David W.

Gihon, James

Gihon, John H.

Gilfry, Samuel

Gibson, James G.

Goodman, John

Grass, George P.

Graham, Wm. D.

Green, R. W.

Greanleaf, Huston

Greaves, Alex.

Grover, Thomas D.

Grossman, E. N.

Gummey, John M.

Harris, William

Harris, Oscar F.

Hay, Peter

Haurmits, John K.

Harmstead, Edward

Hancock, Robt.

Harper, T. E.

Harper, James

Hart, Wm. H.

Harmstead, Geo. R.

Hammitt, Thomas

Hartshorn, Lawrence

Haskell, Ebenezer

Halberstadt, J.

Hallett, Wm.

Hamm, Wm. P.

Hackett, Jos. F.

Hackett, B. E.

Hamilton, W. B.

Hamilton, G. J.

Haines, John

Harned, Joseph E.

Hains, Abraham W.

Hamlin, John L.

Hammitt, Jos. K.

Hand, John K.

Herbert, Charles C.

Herring, Thos. J.
Heysham, Edward
Henzsey, Geo. P.
Henry, William
Hess, John A.
Heiser, H.
Hentzleman, H. P.
Hinman, D. B.
Hiles, Henry J.
Hinckle, Wm.
Hill, George
Hoffner, George
Hopkins, Ambrose
Hornberger, Henry
How, Jacob
Hollinshead, Wm. H.
Horn, Henry
Hollinback, Joseph
Howe, Wm.
Hoffman, Jos. H.
Hollock, George
Hufty, Joseph
Huff, John
Hurtt, Jas. H.
Husbands, Joshua
Hughes, William
Irwin, James
Jack, Charles J.
Jackson, G. W.
Jayne, David
Jarden, William
Jenkins, W. P.

Jenkins, J. G.
Jeffries, Thos. J.
Jones, Charles T.
Jones, Edward E.
Jones, Franklin L.
Jones, John M.
Jordan, E. North
Johnson, N. S.
Kates, Michael
Kerr, Michael
Kern, Wm. H.
Kern, George
Keyser, Elhanan W.
Kennedy, E.
Kennedy, Henry B.
Kelly, Samuel S.
King, Joseph
Kirk, William
Kneider, George
Knight, B. W.
Kramer, Samuel R.
Lasell, Chester
Lancaster, C.
Lafferty, Daniel
Lerbaven, John W.
Lewis, Theo. C.
Levin, Lewis C.
Lees, Jacob
Leinard, Jas. M.
Leech, Isaac E.
Lister, John S.
Linton, John

Lingo, Levi
Lloyd, Joshua
Lloyd, Isaac
Lott, Henry
Long, Peter B.
Lodge, Jacob
Lowdren, Wm.
Lower, Geo. C.
Longacre, Jas. B.
Lowery, Lewis
Luffberry, John B.
Lynch, Urban
Lyndall, Benj.
McCormick, James
McCurdy, John R.
McCully, Henry
McCracken, James
McElroy, J. F.
McFate, Samuel
McGowen, John
McGlathery, James
McIlvaine, Geo. P.
McIntosh, John
McKinley, T. W.
McManus, John
Mandre, Hiram
Markley, Geo. W.
Mayland, Jacob
Maguire, Joseph E.
Massey, Lemuel
Mann, Wm. B.
Martin, Thos.

Martin, Robert C.
March, Robert G.
Mayger, N.
Mason, Geo. W.
Maris, Thomas R.
Mason, Thomas T.
Masson, Chas. H.
Maupay, Samuel
Macpherson, Alex. M.
Meyers, Jacob R.
Mercer, John A.
Meyers, P. R.
Meeser, Christian
Mears, Samuel
Miller, Henry W.
Miller, J.
Miller, P.
Millis, John H.
Mills, John A.
Miles, Wm. S.
Millete, Thomas
Mierclen, J.
Michener, A. C.
Millington, M.
Middleton, Joseph
Middleton, Thos. R.
Miller, Charles
Miles, Henry
Miller, Edward
Moser, Jacob
Morgan, Thos. O.
Moore, Nathan

Moran, William

Moore, David W.

Moore, Wm. R.

Moore, Marmaduke

Moulder, E. S.

Mollincauk, E. P.

Mustin, Ebenezer

Muller, E. M.

Murphy, Wm. D.

Neal, D.

Newman, Jos. K.

Negley, J. R.

Nicholson, James

Nichols, Wm.

Nuttz, E. D.

Oat, Joseph

Odenheimer, G. W.

Oliver, Joshua C.

Ord, John

Orr, Hector

Ord, George

Pancoast, Aaron

Paleske, Lewis

Payne, John

Pachett, George

Paynter, Lemuel

Parsons, Charles R.

Perry, John

Peale, A. R.

Perkins, Thos. J.

Perrine, W. W.

Petit, Edgar E.

Peters, Wm. S.

Peters, James

Peterson, Lawrence

Pfeil, Charles

Phillips, George

Phillips, R. C.

Phillips, A.

Phillips, Wm. James

Pister, John

Plummer, Charles H.

Porter, Stephen

Porter, James W.

Porter, Samuel J.

Poat, Peter M.

Pote, George

Powell, Abraham

Potts, Daniel

Prizer, Peter

Price, Samuel

Prentice, Geo. W.

Quinn, Joseph

Rankin, Alexander C.

Rankin, William B.

Raymond, C. F.

Ragan, William

Ramp, Henry

Reel, Frederick

Reed, George W.

Reed, Henry M.

Rennell, F.

Rheiner, William

Richie, Joseph S.

Richards, William D.
Riley, W. H.
Riley, Jos. S.
Riley, John M.
Ritter, William
Rice, Martin
Rice, William
Rice, George
Rice, Jacob
Rice, John P.
Riter, Michael
Ristine, Jacob
Robinson, Isaac W.
Robinson, William M.
Robinson, J. A.
Roberts, John
Roberts, Robert D.
Rose, Reeves
Rose, Thomas M.
Roat, Jacob
Rowan, C.
Roe, Thomas A.
Robbins, John
Roney, James M.
Rutherford, John
Russell, James
Russell, Henry R.
Salignac, L. T.
Sandeson, William
Sailor, John M.
Salter, Hezekiah A.
Schaffer, W. S.

Schwartz, J.
Sears, Samuel
Sewell, Benjamin T.
Severn, William B.
Setlers, Joseph
Shaffer, Joseph L.
Shaw, M. B.
Shaw, Nathan
Sharp, William W.
Shattuck, Artemus S.
Shankland, W.
Shippen, William
Shotwell, Edward
Shearer, Jacob
Sherman, C.
Sherman, J. R.
Sheetz, William
Sherlock, Parkhurst A.
Shultz, Robert E.
Simons, Henry
Simpson, W. H.
Simpson, Samuel
Simpson, John
Simpson, J. Edward
Simmons, John H.
Simmons, William
Siver, John H.
Skill, John
Slater, Samuel
Slaght, J.
Sloanaker, William
Sleeper, Edwin

Smedley, Nathan
Smith, William G.
Smith, George B.
Smith, Henry L.
Smith, Peter Sken
Smith, Francis
Smith, Jacob C.
Smith, A.
Smith, William R.
Smith, Charles
Smith, J.
Smith, J. W.
Smith, Joshua B.
Smyth, William R.
Snyder, W. G.
Snyder, H. G.
Snyder, Benjamin R.
Souder, William M.
Spear, John D.
Spangler, C. E.
Sparrowhawk, John
Spencer, E. M.
Springer, William F
Stadelman, William
Steever, Edgar G.
Stephens, James H.
Stewart, Henry A.
Stewart, Daniel
Stewart, Reuben
Street, Robert
Stratton, J. B.
Strafford, Jos. B.

Stearley, Jacob
Stiles, William
Stockton, Samuel W.
Strine, Charles
Suber, Aaron
Supplee, John
Swift, H. B.
Sweeds, John
Swip, Henry B.
Tarr, A. De Kalb
Tarr, Elihu D.
Tarr, Henry S.
Taylor, George
Taylor, J. L. S.
Taylor, Thomas
Taylor, George W.
Taggart, Lorenzo
Tabor, J. H.
Tennery, Jos. S.
Thomson, Charles P.
Thomas, Jacob R.
Thomas, Lewis G.
Thompson, David E.
Tillotson, John
Toland, Blair M.
Tolbert, J.
Troutman, L. M.
Tryon, J. G.
Tucker, William E.
Tudor, William
Tyndall, Benjamin
Urwiler, John

Unruh, N. B.
Urwiler, George
Vandusen, Samuel B.
Vaughan, Harman
Vaughan, J. K.
Vaughan, Jacob R.
Vandusen, Matthew
Vandike, William
Van Dyke, James C.
Van Dyke, James M.
Vanderslice, E.
Vice, Martin
Walker, Solomon
Walker, Ambrose
Wagner, Peter
Wands, A. H.
Warner, John S.
Watson, George W.
Wattson, Thomas
Wallace, J. D. F.
Waters, Aaron
Walton, David G.
Waltman, John
Warner, Henry
Waterman, Isaac
Ward, Hiram
Weaver, R. S.
Westcott, Thompson
Wheeler, John
Weiss, George
Wetherell, John M.
West, Washington

West, George G.
Wharton, Charles
Whilldon, Washington
Whittecar, B. W.
White, Philip S.
Williamson, T.
Williamson, J.
Willard, Joseph
Wiley, Charles
Wilson, Charles C.
Wilson, Samuel R.
Wilson, David, G.
Wilson, William
Wise, John
Wise, M.
Wile, John
Williamson, L.
Williams, John S.
Winter, T.
Woods, N. H.
Wood, Thomas A.
Wolf, Lewis C.
Woolmer, Frederick
Woodward, Samuel
Woodington, William
Wright, Peter T.
Yard, Edmund
Yocum, Peter
Yocum, Edward S.
Young, Ezekiel J.
Young, George
Young, Jacob